Music's Duel

Also by Gavin Selerie:

Playground for the Working Line (Ziesing Brothers, 1981)
Azimuth (Binnacle Press, 1984)
Puzzle Canon (Spectacular Diseases, 1986)
Strip Signals (Galloping Dog Press, 1986)
Elizabethan Overhang (Spectacular Diseases, 1989)
Southam Street (New River Project, 1991)
Tilting Square (Binnacle Press, 1992)
Roxy (West House Books, 1996)
Danse Macabre, with Alan Halsey et al
      (Ispress & West House Books, 1997)
Days of '49, with Alan Halsey (West House Books, 1999)
Vitagraph (Binnacle Press, 2001)
Le Fanu's Ghost (Five Seasons Press, 2006)
The Canting Academy, with David Annwn et al (Ispress, 2008)

GAVIN SELERIE

Music's Duel
New and Selected Poems
1972–2008

Shearsman Books
Exeter

Published in the United Kingdom in 2009 by
Shearsman Books Ltd
58 Velwell Road
Exeter EX4 4LD

ISBN 978-1-84861-003-3

Cover image: stained-glass construction by Julie Arnall,
reproduced by permission of the artist.
Digital preparation by Alan Halsey.

CONTENTS

For my niece and nephew
Gemma and Peter

and in memory of my parents
Peter Alexander Shaw Selerie 1916–1989
E. Muriel Helen (Lee) Selerie 1916–2007

One said go
never hesitate

The other said
you will have to stand
by each line
for the rest
of your life

from **Azimuth** (I-IV) *and* **Puzzle Canon**

1972–1978

Star Carr

You stand up a stag,
the skull pressed to your own
with horn-spring
height and hardness,
reaching into the other
dark domain

I was the red deer
I hunted,
I was the year
next given,
I moved above
the marshy lake

Dancing in the campfire flames,
dressed for story-telling,
driven by the load of memory

So the stars shake
the wind cries
the riggs beckon

(Vale of Pickering, 8000 BC)

No Trespassers

Who's here who should not
dwell, them as needs
a scape afar

skin to skin
over ground divide
in secret coppice heart

urgent commune
by orbit turns
to quiet clutch
and let go

rustle, twitch, grunt—
what stirs
under oak and ash
beside strange creature pulse

from the trods
of an ancient ridge
they shift,
dark grey, white heads
streaked with black

bedding to the surface
drag, and nuzzle this soil
for grubs and roots

two feet away
some Doomsday trust
says adult and cubs
will not begrudge
our stay since February
wind by snatches

as the sign, absurd
back there
bears witness

Fyllr

leaning into the hill
she drew him
through green skirt, red knickers

a passage guarded
in modest bud

fear the rays of fire
sixty times a raging child

knitted the several parts
bone blood and limb

Fyllr: or Fulla (filler, lifegiver), handmaiden and confidante
of Frigg. A Norse fertility goddess.

Scope

Reeds, meadows, and sand
reaching flat to the horizon,
scattered farmsteads on low mounds
red above the fields

sky spreading into sea
fixed with ink
murmuring in stillness
across the marshes and dunes

a force agitating from below —
someone walking on the causeway
a faraway giant
the clouds alive with orange
the dykes purple

colour and light
is form itself

Seebüll, 1972

The Ring

We sat silent beneath the moon
in a crown of slender trees
and the legend precipitated
a riot of cordage
from which there could be
no divergence.

Before the chaffinches
a stone curlew
in wild, human voice.
Before the beech-trunks
an oval earthwork,
a later temple
within.

800 feet, a ridge
between the Adur and the Arun,
Celtic banks and hollows.

We looked through silver-grey pillars
towards Cissbury and Lancing,
other crests with a separate music,
towards the tide-pull
at Shoreham.

Leaf and wing forms without I or it
murmur as we drop
steeply from the scarp.
Our feet plot the nervous system
of planets wheeling.
Rabbits scamper in chalk,
flint-flakes shift and scatter,
the field narrows to a tunnel
breathing through foliage.

Sliding more than walking,
we follow a spear point

marked but strange —
a world new, potent, inimical
and besieging: he was talking
of a serpent engendered by the Sun
and killed by him
to protect the human race
who dreaded its fire and suppleness.
Of that same god's pursuit
of a virgin who refused his flame
and was captured in a freeze
of writhing sinews.
He said only: Let her be always
green and shining.

As each tree became that face
and dissolved, moving in and out
of the forest. The years
an elastic turf under foot.

She raises her arms to the stars,
she is fresh as gathered herbs,
she offers new blood for the forgotten,
she is the night prowler's triple dream.

A panel of perforated black,
silver profile of a leering mask.
There was something closed
that began again. He looked ahead
at others ganging. Stopped
as between decades, dim laughter
about. Maybe a trumpet, a trumpet
bottling feeling, a harmon mute
speaking gruffly sweet. Drums
paring each bar with a rimshot.
Tremor on seam of contact.
To each his language — do they know,
can they, is this a non-repeat frame
or a blinker jump?

Flecked forward by a thread
groundlong they go
passing no should or ought
where roots coil like pythons,
branches quiver.

The tall chemist led them back
to the cottage. After him, in line,
the psychologist. Last, as a retina
over crystal, the poet, bringing her power
with him. Down the lane, by hedges
and haystacks, they share thoughts
roughly inherited, take colour
from iron stalks. Quickly the secret
is overlaid: a slippery, thorny track
running south-east between the charted routes.
To the High Street with its curves and dips
and no satyric cries.

Icon of that place, his friend's
woman, she queens it casually
on the doorstep. The cats are roused.

Brushing fat daisies, they walk
as intruders in known space:
the salad on the dresser not for eating,
the disc on the turntable not for hearing,
the books, as a concertina, not for reading.

She turns suddenly and laughs,
her cheeks boned with summer lightning,
and he sees one thought pass over another,
all that was anger being pain.

The head swims with spreading legs
as beams bend in a white room.
Thinking back, he is thinking of a figure
but she reverses
to show a need not voiced
a morning or a season ahead.

She is wearing a red cotton dress
with embroidered mirrors. She has bangles
on her wrist. She drums her fingers
on the couch. Her eyes pierce
a male domain, check-shirted.

Soldiers march across the wall
in green uniforms with red tabs.
A kettle boils after the gas is turned off.
He stubs out a cigarette, eradicating
schooldays. Mud in the crevices
of a boot sole. Daffodils in a Persian
carpet, or lilies expiring. Veins
in an alabaster cup.

What shivers as a tart reply
is not—you stalk the glint
of your own weakness.
A chain unfastens, is there
by the hearth.

One parts the curtains to find a star cluster.
Another feels that rich aggregate,
if ever we were alive, without stirring.
Our silver mistress, constant in change,
sparkles in woodland as the village sleeps.

Hammer Pond

Master Huggett and his man John
They did cast the first can-non

(Sussex Jingle)

Stilled now, the source
which ravaged trees and soil —

Iron, fined, beaten
into grave-slabs, fire-backs,
horseshoes and wheel-tyres

of clanking legions on metalled roads
you can see
when waste, storm-struck
scorches corn

Land that to the Romans
was iron —
beneath silver birches,
bog pimpernel,
lilies-of-the-valley

this small lake where herons and mallard drink,
clearings where deer graze, by beeches,
as herds of wolves and wild boars
did roam

twined branches
over man-dug pits
in old Andredsweald,
divider of east and west

deep holes from which ore was ripped
as, for smelting, tons of wood
were turned to charcoal —
air filled with smoke
and the night ablaze

heads of water,
ghylls diverted and dammed,
driving the great hammers
and bellows

till 1648
when Cromwell sent a force
to silence the works

traces of charcoal and cinder
beneath pine needles and leaves

like the names:
Furnace Pond
Cinder Banks
Hammer-hill wood

The True Generation of Serpents

In Sussex there is a pretty market-towne called Horsam, and neare unto it a forrest called St Leonard's Forrest, for that lilies sprang up where this saint's blood fell in his combate with a strange & monstrous serpent which attacked him.

There is an unfrequented place, heathie, vaultie, full of unwholesome shades and over-growne hollowes, where this serpent is thought to be bred; but, wheresoever bred, certaine and too true it is that there it yet lives. Within three or four miles compasse are its usual haunts, oftentimes at a place called Faygate, and it hath been seene within halfe a mile of Horsam; a wonder, no doubt, most terrible and noisome to the inhabitants thereabouts. There is always in his tracke or path left a glutinous and slimie matter (as by a small similitude we may perceive in a snaile's) which is very corrupt and offensive to the scent.

The serpent (or dragon, as some call it) is reputed to be nine feete, or rather more, in length, and shaped almost in the forme of an axletree of a cart; a quantitie of thickness in the middest, and somewhat smaller at both endes. The former part, which he shootes forth as a necke, is supposed to be an elle long; with a white ring, as it were, of scales about it. The scales along his backe seem to be blackish, and so much as is discovered under his bellie appeareth to be red; for I speak of no nearer description than of a reasonable ocular distance. For coming too neare it, hath already beene too dearely payd for.

It is likewise discovered to have large feete, but the eye may be there deceived; for some suppose that serpents have no feete. He rids away (as we call it) as fast as a man can run. He is of countenance very proud, and at the sight or hearing of men or cattel, will raise his necke upright, and seem to listen and looke about with great arrogancy. There are likewise upon either side of him discovered, two great bunches so big as a large foote-ball, and (as some thinke) will in time grow to wings; but God, I hope, will destroy him before he grow so fledge.

He will cast his venome about four rodde from him, as by woefull experience it was proved on the bodies of a man and woman comming that way, who afterwards were found dead, being poysoned and very much swelled, but not prayed upon. Likewise a man going to chase it and, as he imagined, to destroy it with two mastive dogs, as yet not knowing the great danger of it, his dogs were both killed, and he himselfe glad to returne with hast to preserve his own life. Yet this is to be noted, that the dogs were not prayed upon, but slaine and left whole; for his food is thought to be, for the most part, in a conie-warren, which he much frequents; and it is found much scanted and impaired in the encrease it had woont to afford.

The persons, whose names are hereunder printed, have seene this serpent, beside divers others, as the carrier of Horsam, who lieth at the White Horse in Southwarke, and who can certifie the truth of all that has been here related, this present Month of August, 1614.

> John Steele
> Christopher Holder
> and a Widow Woman dwelling nere Faygate

This legend my old friend Dr. Mantell, the geologist, used to quote as possibly to be traced to the Saurians, whose fossil remains are now to be found abundantly in the neighbouring beds of Tilgate Forest. — Draco (1878)

The Knucker

From a bottomless pond in the Lancing flats
the water beast rises, horselike, its conical head
querulous, twisting from a tall thin body
to gobble cattle, interrupt business.

It is the charge, the ocean breaching chalk
as our ancestors cry to be known — a gallop
through black, silver, crimson, before diving
without a trace beneath the surface.

The pool is cold in summer but never freezes
in frost, for then it gives off a vapour,
being warmer than the air. To take one breath,
one draught, may stir hunger in the coils below.

What did I do with my school compasses
and protractor, kept in a long thin box
upon which I scratched, over the *Oxford* scene
some picture of dumb-bell oak, the quad
and Johnnie Walker's walking stick,
aged thirteen, as if to hold on
among the polished brasses
and spooned toecaps —
or more probably to find my way out
with Latin and Edwardian marches
inside.

Nine miles in the wrong direction
we went, after the commander
read this chart backwards
and we camped out on Black stichel
like Douglas, without even a bracken-bush.

Where to go without denying a whole life
of roaring voices and swaggering.

In 1917, to a thatched cottage
off a secluded winding lane
which runs from Fittleworth to Wisborough Green:

Writing from a studio in the garden,
'I get Beer here in plural quantities.
It seems strange after the difficulties
of London . . . It is lovely to hear the birds —

nightingales abound and their song is really
the most lovely thing in nature.
I feel like these words all aglow —
a spark would start a flame
and no human spark comes.'

Chamber music after the hurly-burly,
piano and violin his working instruments.

A wine glass will have to do tonight,
or several with different bases.
Botching and parti-coloured is it
we are or grow to be?

In Shoreham

The sea has always been regarded by coastal and seafaring peoples as the ideal place for dumping their waste and this is, of course, a very reasonable and proper attitude. (Almost everything put into the sea is either diluted or broken down or stored harmlessly on the sea bed.) Most of the objects which ultimately do find their way to the shore are harmless and a considerable source of pleasure to children. Not the least of the attractions of the sea as a dumping ground has been the lack of administrative controls.

John Dunster, Chief Health Physicist,
Windscale, UN conference report

Often I must vie with the wave and fight with the wind,
contend with them combined, when, covered by surf,
I go to ground; my own country seems foreign.
If I become still, I am staunch in the struggle;
if I fail to be so, they are stronger than I am
and, through tearing, soon put me to flight,
wishing to carry off what I must protect.
I can foil them if my tail endures
and if the stones hold firm against my grasp,
that hard iron-bite. Ask what my name is.

from the *Exeter Book*

Demijohn

for Marija Gimbutas and Elizabeth Van Buren

A myth is it? the proper grace —
did not behave and skewed the data.
Muffled in silence over and over, she said,
the whole mental thing, the whole physical bit,
the lot in fact has been completely different.

Like in an old Marine Dictionary
it was *dame-jeanne*, or Lady Jane,
meaning that the water jar
with its rounded body and small neck
was cave and house, or in other terms
the milk from heaven.

The mother liquid pouring forth,
sometimes in pain or difficulty,
to make things grow and ripen.
Clothed with wicker or rush-work,
hands resting on her abdomen,
she might seem a kind of property,
white foam nearing land.

In Egypt she was slim, in Malta fat,
in Cyprus she had pierced ears,
in Phoenicia, large round eyes.
Crete gave her snakes to hold.
In the Cyclades she was a cello,
in Britanny and Ireland, a rayed circle
cut into rock.

They made her what they wanted:
guardian of lambs,
watcher by the fireside,
blessed healer,
bringer of peace,
guide for wanderers.

Part of her in the brothel,
part in the marriage bed —
Astarte, Venus, Freya
or Lily Marlene.

Listening and weighing what others say,
she's all of these and excluded
from thought, a person whose name
is double glazed to deny
any breath of origin.

The dot in the lozenge

Brings of herself
the blade, the ear, the full corn.

Clothed with the sun,
crowned with the stars,
moon underfoot,
but split into halves
(scarlet and white)
by police post eyes.

Speech robbed into soul
keeps as it is
a guess.

That not impossible ardent stunner
rigged out fond and fleet
to be there, tasting
sweet as summer rain.

Darling! as she bends her head
shocking you *****
a modern, sensuous fragrance.

What it did for them
it can do for you.

Encounter the stars/cut-price chic
says a lot for you/they're not false
just me and a great new/natural local
hydrotherapy/the High Gloss look/
Slendertone. Because/win a smooth
automatic/tingling fresh and prettier,
smoother, more comfortable with no
complicated routines/Lovable all
underneath/one shouldered tree-bark
satin/Get the soft, moist pucker.

I did actually rather want to
have a drink. Is anything
that simple? the sign
that stands for something
to somebody, you say.
Suddenly-seen things
that were always there:
through it all
the object alive
as your own reflection, man.

De Luce

He held the bulb

moved as a butterfly
in her nectary

lady of the field
a Turk's Cap

loosing, redeeming,
ransoming

of fleshy scales
without a tunic,
leaves borne
on the aerial of the stem
whorled, purple
flowers erect
to nodding

not of sorrow
or the shortest day
but of the east
(as Horus)

Was by the pond is inside the silt,   clean   clear
Is fingering the stalk was there   no tree branching
tiptoeing on the slats of the tiny bridge We they
were are   at a great distance laughing   the birds
no idea stay   held in sanctuary   inside her diadem
of him   a domed liquid steering   No others to ask
in that place   marine-wood   peer through rhododendron
her Alpine rose   there is no hunger or edge   there is
the ground as a cylinder   stroking sky-words   her
blue corduroy dress   softening, unravelling   a plot
the resolution of one vowel into two   and its solution
the banquet of tongue, palm   out through silky spheres
black lustring   out to the vast
beyond

to dissolve or liquefy

made by the breaking down
of neighbour-cells
of ethereal oil in plants

(a crystalline compound

origin of the reservoirs

of raging love the goddess
or worm under the tongue
of dogs

Desire madly to   the yellow or golden willow herb
of rest, leaves spotted with black —
Lysimachia or Loosestrife
bees disclose in summer

thrusting into spiked cups
revellers buried in a disc

yield to others that feed

Lyein   thought lines wash   moreyne
Lysine   abate without crisis

Inside your head there are two of us she said, the whole
matter in a flash   cupping the soil in each hand
leaning forward   and her skin went white   as her eyes
retreated

moves the boat on water   I came towards the water/
as the shore sails   me came from surface

we bridge-sang   sounds as we crossed

she bent to touch the tubers embedded in mud, the dress
was long-stalked circular leaves, the dress was a shield,
the leaf and flower   air passages

the stem was hard,   I-by-man-see, by me
the parts bind,   a man is seen, I see
the position   a man, by-me-man-plural
presented   see
the feel
                       the leaf is soft
an aura of self-outsurge   at this moment
the plant-man-woman   between fingers
between   and the stem-born
                       parents bud in its angle

She said, I want to know but I don't want to take
the petals apart. This I want to know without being

the subject of seeing. This is me, I am it, we are
in each other. The water has no mind to receive our image.
I have no mind to truly think. Our eyes see the lotus
Egyptian-white

without gloss   you slot into place
night-blooming

These flowers   most open of day
are of themselves and us we see

Bridge thunderingly silent,
strikes a light-flash
signet-ripple
                              Touching him for refutation
for the twigs and leaves vaporized, for the father
who watches from windows and tapestries

                        Her irises rolled upwards—
he says you are your self to hold in me. She reached
for the path, watched her footsteps returning,
the browns gliding solid, the greens a fretwork shimmer.
She walked with them as not herself
held hands.

The world sings (*lila, lie-la-lie*) oozily

Up from the ground where limbs brush their faces
a woman, a man unfold, skin shining. Smeared,
swaying branches avail a way, the earth webbed
with root and ditch folds. As birds warble or trill,
as insects crawl, this holt breathes, sun-spoked,
its bloodstream lapping close and far-off
rim to core

                    They turn
                    before
                    the fence, ivy-laced.
                    A plantation is human hair,

fibres half-heavy hang,
tips alert

They gaze at their goodbye figures,
at the gauzy, secret drive
of all about

As preverbal children
nothing stands that is not here—
they are the slow pour
of viscid life,
the fluting of errant colours
to focus

Hands curled loosely
as fallen petals,
the idea is the form inside:
a vermilion field,
a cobalt breeze

Shapes
tower, undulate
from open hour-book,
the clearing
heavy with scent

They drink cold silver,
avoid the tarmac,
wind back
to houses
and ordered gardens

The path is patterned
with black fronds,
a white seam
connects
the three-parted capsule,
the growing edge,
the times

Untitled

I deny the accident
moving inside the line
which flows over margins

I am a female clown
sitting on a flower
which is also the sun

my bottle the moon
snakes across your wall

now a mask or minotaur
knotted

space hollows itself out
image turning to image
upon an unprimed, porous surface

The buffalo woman
trying to spring out
of vegetation

the tendril a tendon

After the effort of the dance
the thickness of white
the cat with horns

I like to be literally
in the painting

the painting has a life
of its own

I try to let it come
through

Botanologia

Of fellow creatures, strange
  and close, the eye/hand
    between sets
        do read

        disposure
        potency
        resemblance

        catmint, kin to alehoof,
        bishopweed

flaunting yellow goatsbeard,
clump of Solomon's seal

        ox-eye daisies,
        shaggy parasol

bellflower, bats in the belfry,
blossom of blackthorn

        velvet dock,
        cuckoo spit

smell smock,
lady's bedstraw

        nipplewort,
        clover knob

Cull me to you/record
    in situ, performance
            neck bent

            to rise
        a vulgar/fine
memo-chanter

Stake and let go—
conglobation of bubbles,
pond-skater in a silver coat of air

lilac leaf-miner
pharaoh's ant
water-boatman
pear-midge
leather-jacket
ghost swift
oak-egger
pinhole borer
devil's coach horse
hairy summer chafer

Name to know the several bodies
in walked ground or water
all a story to recite

Not the rapture
of lawns and parks
blended features to preserve

but quaking and trembling soil
buffeting to compute
virtues secret
inside

Scarp Stubbs

Dawn above Coxwold
where we have lain all night
a figure cut out
of the hillside

sandstone warming
and prinked with skylarks
after moth wings, ant's feet
and moist star-breath

Rosedale

1

Over heather and ironstone
down the chimney bank, sheer
to the circle and basin,
holy ground
with nested precincts,
a nine mile furrow
ploughed by a giant

hrossa-dair, horse valley
we tumbled
through

notched slabs
with lambs frisking,
a rule of white in the veins

no high ruin
to show
where these ladies walked

did they
on this spiral staircase
hear music

the brass even
that is now
Sunday

soft where I want
to lay my head
beneath the sycamore

2

Glass Holes
a little way south
in shale and sandstone

dug for rabbits
yield something else

vessels
from a winged furnace
under bracken

pale green beaker pieces,
neck of a wrythen Kuttrolf bottle,
pincered handle from a bleeding bowl,
girth of a globular jug,
linen-smoothers or slick-stones

Allen (allemain?) House,
roofless cottage
last used as a byre

a burnt stone below the step,
sherds and a scatter of rubble
outside

3

The chimney is a ghost
on the Dogger
tall over grouse
by the reservoir,
taken three years back

Slag and charcoal
near the abbey (nunnery)
clinch what's told
in the charter —

right to gather wood
and smelt ore

a bell pit, precarious
dug into the seam
to feed a bloomery,
this and later shafts
overgrown

centuries are here to clamber
anti-clockwise

gable end — Pit Manager's
house — a jagged tooth,
arched row of roasting kilns,
drift entrance with headroom,
a length of track still,
bent axle of a runaway wagon

who at a cost will draw
the perfect nugget

scrape in foul air,
moleskin and flannel
against smoky flame,
miners' beds
never cold
as shift replaces shift

about the sides we wind
in disjointedness and moulder
a reading comes
clear

Shandy Shivers

Hollo, ho! a two-mile walk
over Brink Hill   trod a hundred times

to pluck a score of briars
by the roots   find Cordelia

wheel of west front
broken   lune-gaze

over tiles geometric
green and yellow   candle blood

lozenge to spiral
twisting a lock   asylum shade

> There's nothing in the map
> so like — did you narrowly
> look — her name & picture —
> a translator can't say much
> in this bye-corner — but let
> the mind vibrate — curious
> traveller — through the field
> to another gate — it's as real
> as any space — or chapter of
> chances — a feeling mocked
> from the first letter — warm
> at the core of hardened jest.
> Why should she not remain
> fresher than mosaic to clasp

Aversion

As he bent to show us
the working of the presses
in 1600, with text hollered down
from floor to floor
and a screw to force the platen down,
a woman with a thick accent
said to her boys,
Don't look at these —
they're instruments
of torture.

Transmission

Ouse river wharf evening sun sink,
north look Rosedale, not see home.
Bell ring several noise, sky-earth
float float clapper out/Goodmanham

Cause and Effect

sin

cynical

cinders

Of Mausolus

Let Monuments and rich Fabricks, not Riches adorn
mens ashes. The commerce of the living is not to be
transferred unto the dead.

    Sir Thomas Browne, Hydriotaphia: Urne-Buriall

Gout — Gout. Grim palisade
in Yeomans Close, Dec. 1723. Gout.
A belvedere after the antique
(vid. Herodotus, Pliny, and M. Varo)
built all with ruff stone
to keep off filth, the living
and lighten the dead within.

Chalk quarries in his stomach
and the making nearly all
by letter, 200 miles and more.

Experience and trials.
(We shall not know where
it will end, a doubter said,
of All Souls.)

The shape come from
occasion, materials, land
as bone-blazon, parts
complete, whatever bluff
in his justification,
the years told.

Spring on the brink
of a steep balk, no shiver
in the lake beside.

I was at iron gates,
the hill I stepped up
massing dark against sky:
drum and dome, rising

from another, wider,
its columns crowded
with Artemesia's yearning.

I reached out
a form and figure durable
if anything is so
in this world.

Away from all commerce,
worship even, the cherubs' heads
and flowers in the cap of
this cell, the panelled circles
you tread on, the loculi
bedded below.

Remote impress of honey,
the doorcases do not lead
out, our coming and going
in round, quietness
fortified and high.

Sol in a crocus, a daffodil,
back through fields, across water
I did somehow walk
to other confinements.

A peacock cries shrill—
I thought could never
fly—from the lime branches.

Versipellis

Moor folded against moor,
a purple sea, ghosts
in the throat,
a glint of polar
desire

chant the quickness of godflesh
its red with white warts
dried and chewed

wood-men
scenting lineage
convulsive
formation
like hardening
the body below
best bearing torment

dream coat
molars
through fire and iron

a sulphur seed
did we implant

for one reeling wedding
froth beat
beyond parlour games
of ivory fingers

this *vargrant* spirit
in smoke
on a railed stair
says take
over wait

cut the blood-eagle
in a city square
as cameras jam
and buttons clink

end of a start
bannered, daubed
under spire
by husky tongue

so you pass
bone, tendon, nerve
between states

touched with the spear
to go lamp-eyed
on the long trail
or lie in cut banks
with leaves and moss

then after nine years
re-swim the lake
for human clothes
hanging from an oak

to leave and regain
the band

Greenhouse

for Sue Ferrar

Lines of glass and concrete
on a marsh drained, as hyperspace
to stop Ford setting another northern plant
here, the city fathers wanted quiet
and the pay battened fast.
Only the library, built to last
fifty years, is not sinking
into the lake. By a steel cloister
incorporating board, one avoids
the rain, steps toward
wild swans by a Jacobean hall
where the purse strings hang.
As they built each college
the rooms got smaller.

Bodies bunged up with a cork
and speech grit found only in the network:
Tam o'Shanter and now the Spreadeagle
a circle around the city
out from Mount Parade or Alligator
to Ash Tree House, Skewsby,
Grange Farm, the Lodge at Escrick.
Squatted the land and lived
by the old tongue and candlelight,
sharing a clownish pulse,
light and loose to shake the scene.
Farmers surprised might smile
where agents would cling to a statute.
Drove up through the mud,
ruts a constant path, hens clucking.
Walked in through the window,
sleeping all night in hay. Make and get
parsnip roast, a guitar and flagons of wine:
a canticle for the new Elizabethans —
even the motorcycle with a coffin

as sidecar. As a poet might desire,
the Vatican library
dropped in the Amazon jungle.

The Rose

Through the West window
the sun cuts dust, traces
a pageant on flagstones.
A maiden opening to the glance
of heaven, embraces a warrior
to rise out of chaos. Yielding
cinnamon and myrrh, she twists him
gloriously in darkness,
offers fruit, grace, rhythm
to sons of the divider.
Flashed or enamelled,
fitted into channelled lead
and set in an iron frame,
the veined leaf or spoked wheel
was entirely conceived
at the bench — a jewel
that surprised even the maker.

Stump-Work

Out here with her, nimble and trim,
the support of every root and vein,
how all stretches in accord
from sap strong shoots to a lubric bird.

> black maidenhair
> naked ladies
> pissabed
> mares fart
> priest's ballacks
> horse pistle
> prick madam
> open arse
> twitch-ballock
> bum-towel

This herb is called Maiden hair
or waterwort. This herb hath leaves
like to Fern, but the leaves be smaller,
and it groweth on walls and stones,
and in the midst of the leaf
is as it were black hair.

What a volume of vocabularies might tell
or entertainment at the village fête —

> a horse's head painted before him
> and a tail behind, and the whole
> covered with a long foot-cloth,
> as if to hide an animal body,
> ambles, prances, plunges

Clownish, scrambling antic
talk with fingers the first O, niddety nod
to ribbons and bells leap. Side over
side the parts twangle. Whose
sleeve and hood are these?

At the spinney edge
you may delve but never catch.

        sometime comes a great Blacke dog
        sometime flying like a Sparrowe
        with a Woodcocks bill
        sometime creeps a Toade
        with a nose like a Moale
        sometime like a Mouse
        sometime like a Minister
        sometimes an Ey without a head
        above all with a drumme
        and seaven motly vizards

Outline stitched, read more
the heart, not so secret to find
lichen-vested trees with moss footing,
scarred arms in still, slow combat,
lobes of fungi, rotting shroud
spongy beneath.

Elsewhere is a bole which weeps rosin—
can this be held in our catalogue?

        from the root, hard and ruff
        grows a single stem, orbicular,
        canelike, whitish within,
        hollow like the stem of Allisander,
        nicked and notched
        after the manner of Pillars,
        full of Threds or Hairs like Strings
        in which consists the chief Value
        and Dignity of the herb
        whose height may surpass
        the length of a Lance

Taking the picture away by getting inside
as today the wild works. No overlapping
seasons here and ground is occupied:

tufts of green catkin-flowers
to ripen into yellow-brown keys.

Ash burns fierce while it is green,
I told her, as people pressed to see.

Rievaulx

Oh how she flings her arms and smiles
as men never do, walking in these woods
with the scent of purple and white garlic
on a Sunday with not a soul around.

Catching her look I think,
the abbey reaches up from Ryedale:
upstanding fragments of a damp existence,
placed so as to deny the careless life,
where labour is prayer, a cellular quest
to drive wolves, wild cats away,
hear only thrushes and sheep.
No heat except two braziers of charcoal
in the common-room and kitchen.

Then the place is a buzzing hive
with hundreds of monks and brothers —
the white order, with simple dress and food,
in wild country, as always
with a good supply of water.
Each according to his knack, a pioneer
to hold these blocks together —
stark by example of wealth
the refectory raised upon a vaulted cellar
in which provisions are stored.
Knew every stone in the scheme,
a master-mason using the fall of ground.

Solitary, all stages of the structure showing,
from the marrow to the white robe
covering delicate parts.

Grass in the choir and transepts
inside of which we move, gently, as
light ascending to heaven, a winged demon
along filleted triple vaulting-shafts,
rhythming limbs from arcade piers

to the gallery, with stiff-leaf and hood mould,
plain severity thrown to the wind.

Gone back, as a sketch to the finished picture,
it is rough-dark beyond smoother surfaces—
buildings aligned north to south with the land
and only half-human now
as belemnite exposed in the thigh.

In this piece of moulding
the man and woman seem to be flying
and a frieze shows a horse
bringing sacks of corn to a windmill.
Are these cinders
from a hammersmithy for shears?
Staple evidence—
wool and iron beneath a crown
of high hills.

North we come to get wood from the forest,
fuel for a week ahead,
but here is our school of love
and link to the centre. Roof lead surviving
in the Five Sisters window.

Garland

for Alan Halsey

Was out on the street, the word
that made us come across
and get a piece of that life,
so it's no longer a safety-valve
pushed into another time
or confined to holy days.

To speak in Saxon, do make it
a common storehouse for all:
do away with tithes and tolls,
the whole damn lot o'them.

Got into that rotation, doing smoke —
an emission from the devil's forge,
hah, those hot letters in the hands
of the composer, got it out real quick.

Simple and mean things
to confound the mighty and strong,
like you'd trust a thief
more than a priest or lawyer.

Dig and level, to let every one
quietly have earth to manure,
working the forests and wastes,
eating bread together.

Thinking it out and playing the parts:
planted carrots, parsnips, beans
to keep the cattle alive through winter
and so fertilize the land.

The earth our birthright,
being in her, flowers round the pole,
her voice of calm encouragement
a blast of joy in spring again.

Christ a corn of wheat
buried under clods
for a time
to rise on this.

Adam before our eyes
walking up and down the street:
the whims of tipsy topsy-turvydom
knit into one. Maydays — overnight
Took: a futurists' drum.

Barricade Music

for Phil Ochs (1940–1976)

Sitting in a booth in Imhoffs, 1966
jotting down the words of songs
I couldn't afford to buy.
Snatched meetings on every journey
from home to school. *In Concert*
was the one, real despite the pacing,
with Mao's poems on the sleeve,
the guitar a bayonet of peace —
I'm going to say it now.
Marines landing on the shores
of San Domingo.

Then in Old Town, 1968
running from bums and thieves on Clark Street,
I found a promo copy of *Pleasures*,
the sea-dog returning from Liverpool,
Mayorga's piano no obvious Hollywood
hokum, no sentimental love bilge.
My first rites with the woman
who had means to reproduce it.
The sky alight on the South Side,
I have a dream cut by guardsmen and curfew,
like a server rewriting the record.

Coffeehouses, festivals, rallies,
you took the war in your teeth,
jammed a torch in the face of Mississippi,
walked the line in Hazard, Kentucky.
With laughter in each strike,
that was the key. *Prologue*:
the only folksinger in Chicago
with Hoffman and Rubin
trying to get a sound truck
to demonstrate with dignity
before the baton charge.

Regarded with amusement, said the journal
—*Guess I'll have to do it while I'm here.*
Writing from the headlines
on to a trusted frame.

Obliquely the bard who survives
lace fog in Lincoln Park
makes this suffering land a woman
with flaming eyes
lately turned to stone.

You were on the lam, William Butler Yeats
freaked by a bitter feast.

While we were dancing
you threw psychedelia in the pool,
saw the conspiracy to silence
each breath. As if behind the revel
Viva Zapata was showing
a fight for the sun
whose take is our shadow alone.

Yet, no puritan, Ché in a lamé suit
might reach the workers.
Now Holly or Presley
you sought out the airways
with songs that track high noon,
a golden throat, a satin medley
and still the critic's bite.

At Carnegie Hall a voice from the back
shouted *the one we knew is dead.*
El Paso to the Village,
Chicago to the Hollywood hills.

Then into exile: Chile, Tanzania,
a song in Swahili and Lingala,
a concert for blacks in Witwatersrand.

They tried to keep him quiet:
a TV ban, deported from Dublin
at the CIA's request.
In Dar es Salam, the year Jara was murdered,
they hired thugs to stop his voice —
the larynx, without cutting the jugular,
three top notes.

A ticket home to the movie town:
Not only did I continue drinking,
I ripped out their sink.
In Lenny's vomit-stained jacket
a new persona, John Butler Train
crashing anywhere.

Cynicism: a cloak for passion
jerked back, the drive that always
wants one touch.

Returning to Gerde's Folk City:
You better use the knife or I will,
the last phase — only other people's songs
like Big Iron and Too Many Parties.

Far Rockaway, New York, with his own belt
in his sister's bathroom
ripped the chords of fame
as he had rehearsed it
in diagonal paces on Prince Street.

The best raconteur, spirit strong,
it was they say an age ahead
dreaming with him.

July Wakes

for Leo Kottke

Start with a box but it's your hand
does it, the strum of wheels rolling
with a rasp, a blur to something finer,
this green snake a distant curve
with diamond eyes.

Telegraph wires in the mist, flicker
of hotel voices. High girders
over water, daredevil ruse. Tunnel smoke
filling the compartment, pinprick of light,
a cardplayer knocked to the floor.

The notes come in a twirl, a throb, a twang
from Athens, Georgia to Minneapolis
then back to East Virginia with accent
pushed through the nose to cut grass.
Against a window of states
without the high end of hearing
you squint as lines converge
and splay apart.

Scenes spin as a circus
with the top blown off—
ribbed Scarlatti, a lady in the doorway,
children playing leapfrog on the courthouse steps.
Scud and slide of a june bug, secrets stuffed
in a bureau drawer, teen-fierce embrace
behind the church, bank clerk fixed
to the bar. Figures down the beam
of one sentence dance a bourrée
and settle in a rocking chair.
Imitation of all you ever heard
by shotgun shacks beneath a jonquil sky.

Truth could be the first take,
it's less an attempt at being good.

Keep the rough edges, don't lose the wood.
Tune two steps below concert pitch
to save the strings from stress.

Lying in the Lancashire mud
I ask for Lady Margaret. Oh *that?*
Slipped away like the Gibson 12-string
stolen from the back seat of my car in '69.
I've found the same model and year
and everything since
but there's no *definition* —
which is what sound is about.

The Tyger

There never was any public or saloon —
just front and back, cut by the generations:
the elders playing dominoes with a TV hum,
rockers and communists in a drinking truce.
No heating in winter but Old Brewery
through clean pipes, gie me that,
a likely young lass, eh? wer niver,
they dunnot tell thee it were riven,
I never thought but you'd pick a winner,
nowt fro'th'field in his house . . .
where the devil is the use on't?

With the landlord's pate and belly
two beaming markers, pulling the pints
till twelve, anecdotes crossing the floor,
a flash of vaudeville kickin to the roots:
Latest Flame, Um Oh Yeah, and Memphis Tennessee,
farm lads rocketing off into the night,
a few bottles through the window
of an empty cottage, still hearing that riff.

When they brought in hunting horns
and dial-a-tone patter, when beer mat circles
gave way to eight-seaters and minute steak,
George was relieved and became a pump attendant,
the sign was repainted on a larger board
and jungle roots were shoved beneath a smile.

Then the saloons swept in, laminated:
some on the sidelines, nervous cool,
others preening behind moustaches and makeup.
Oh you needn't thank me, Polly,
I say the same of you sometimes
and I think it too.

We still went there dammit,
though we fended off the jugs.

Stairway

i.m. A. [S.] D., April 1978

Saw you walking, a chorale
on the morning heave,
a hind on a ridge of grey
and you said it was not you.

The ocean draws our memory
from our mind.

We don't want other worlds,
we want a mirror of our own.

You slipped like Mary Stuart
(sang your own epitaph)
but in that tower by water
you could sing full force
into a candle flame
without a waver or sigh.

Amsterdam perhaps,
you made it from the clubs
and bars, in ardour
to a long gown and no guitar.

I always smoke them down
to the word, it all comes out
as hymn tunes.

I was curious to see what
would happen,
that was all.

If you don't know the lyrics
the sense is plain enough:

a queen among the heather,
wishes scaled to naught.

It doesn't take long to kill things,
not like it does to grow.

from Azimuth (V-VII) *and* Puzzle Canon

1978-1984

As Herodotus

We followed the royal road
from Sardis, lying at night
in well provided inns,
till we hit the Euphrates
spanned by a city
larger even than Nineveh:
Mother of Harlots,
clothed in fine linen,
purple and scarlet,
decked with gold and pearls.
By the tawny waters
we thought of populous lands
left for the ass and gazelle,
of fruit-trees, gardens, canals
scorched by the sword of Nergal.
And rising above the plain
in eight stages, Bel's ladder
to the dome of heaven. We saw
people of many races thronging,
their faces black with heat.
A horse reared, talents scattered,
the whip cracked a thief's only reach.
In procession, the way flanked
with lions, we entered the Ishtar gate
where bulls and dragons spoke
of the Morning-Evening star
raining naptha over Arabia.
Along a limestone pavement cut with words
on the buried side, past the edge
of breccia slabs, veined red and white,
we drove to the ziggurat,
a mountain plated with gold
and blue enamelled brick —
a terrace of fifty million blocks.
Arrogance: the lion crushing the builder,
22 tons of gold on a golden throne —
Marduk seated — does not confirm belief.

No one but a chosen woman
inhabits the pinnacle
to do his pleasure
on a warm couch.
Behind us now the hanging gardens
cunningly balanced over a vaulted crypt,
arches that swing water up and down.
Then westward across the river,
frankincense drifting from the grid
of streets, wool draped from balconies.

Once in her life, every woman
native to the country
must go to Aphrodite's temple
and give herself
to a strange man.

But the King will fall (*synodos*)
from the heights
like a morning star

And certain refugees
will flee to Egypt
attributing red tumult
to their desertion
of the planetary gods,
especially Venus,
Queen of Heaven.

A Meeting with the Doctor

Get rid of your abstract nouns he said
they seem to aim at heaven
but only weigh you down.

Take an object
feel it
as an Anglo-Saxon riddle.

I am the colour of blood
was once a thrust among many.
Men rent me worse than the wind
but trained me to help others grow.

I turn more, am less round.

Remember
the eye
will follow
eagerly

when a rune
speaks
for
itself.

Watching the night sky
with her in my arms,
April grasses underfoot

Berenice's hair clustered loose:
a thousand strands
in token of safe return

Arcturus light orange
from the curve
of the Great Bear's tail

Regulus white —
the dot of a question mark
or sickle-grip

Draco winding its way,
a faint trail
from the Pointers to Vega

a recognizable darkness,
her fire rings
the hint of tomorrow's countenance

Ohne

did not confine their gods
within walls did not
make images of them
but rather consecrated
forests and groves
calling by the names
of gods that *secretum*
which they beheld only
with the reverence
of their own eyes

after Tacitus, *Germania*, IX

Paris 1912

We spend our lives trying to construct sentences,
then ache to undo them when action will not fit
the mood. I told her things I did not mean,
she said a doll, dismantled to the tune of a tango:
nine to five, driving at seventy in the middle lane,
cramming more hours into the day. I saw her
pear-chopped beneath the girdered sky,
a bunch of bananas in the square, sprouting
from beside her torso. I wanted to say,
I meant to say, I always said, there is this wish,
egg, pipe, ball, rod, emblems of play
in a sailor's barracks. You come as a shadow
beneath the tower, the arches,
a muse with harlequin boxes and cylinders.
I have my canvas, framed. There is the smoke
of a train leaving, puffs as fish
in the living room. The scholar waits,
a balloon beckons. I take the words apart
in imitation of the dream.

Orlando

In back chambers with ornate panelling
marked by rocks, trees and figures
that glided silver on stage,
he made fantasies for the keyboard
and played for nine yards of blacks
the well-known theme
in a web of counterpoint:

> rosiness an emblem
> of change and secrecy

> with cries of London,
> her oysters in a cobbled market

> murmurings behind a line of oaks,
> take comfit cake, cordial from his cup

The best hand in England,
Chamberlain averred
after the fit
took him

> (wrung his mouth to his ears,
> a fifth augmented
> on the word
> as in drumly revels)

elegiac after the velvet age,
a pyramid circled with all store
of light.

How they danced and commoned together
lustily, with joy.
How they made their faces known
and departed.
How soprano and viols
stay to record
the blooming
zeal and blushes.

Habitaculum

The case, box, stand	from which to look
	to gain one's bearings
	to have hold of
	in a settled condition

| I went up to the loft | was rotten   saw through |
| | the rafters and slates |

I went down into	
the cellar	tunnels stretching
	under the street
	damp black spaces
	for rats to crawl

substrata	the germinal cell or sac
	where a translator
	begins his work
seed of fire	in a furnace
Golden Flower	that blisters to fruition
out of lead	about the water-region.

Gin bottles under the floorboards, crammed
into the cistern, so her husband wouldn't know
her dreams.

James Thomson, progenitor of the estate
lived to see his houses shine but left — as gamblers
at the Hippodrome lost — just £789 at death.
Nos. 98–104 even, leased by C.H. Blake
to Edmund & Elias Cordery of Bayswater, builders, 1860.
The 1863–5 survey shows dwellings up to 104.
North of that the land is vacant.

Coming back to the old charts it is plain
that a boundary exists right here: a jutting wedge
of the St. Quintin estate which Blake had to take
to provide access to the northern part

of his Portobello estate. So the Grove is extended north
of Ladbroke Estate, diagonal at a slight swerve.
December 1864: Blake signs a contract
with Col. Matthew Chitty Downes St. Quintin
of Lowthorpe & Scampston Hall, Yorks, ground landlord.
The covenant to build at least seven shops,
each to be worth not less than £700,
and at least fifty-four houses, each of £1,200 in value.
To submit all plans and elevations for approval,
to comply with structural conditions
and to complete the programme within four years.
In return, St. Quintin grants him ninety-nine year leases
at a peppercorn rent for the first twenty-one months
and then at £610 per annum, equal to the ground rental
of c. £152 per acre.
Blake keeps his bargain along the main road,
putting up buildings *of character*, as also
along the transverse streets.
But as early as 1868, St. Quintin's agent
threatens to deny access to the Portobello estate
unless arrangements are come to
regulating the class of houses
to be erected on Blake's property.
But from Ireland and Africa they'll come
and the lines are the same today —
drinking haunts and a carnival on tarmac.

Sometime in the late sixties they put this one up —
first reference in the census of 1871:

106	Louis Krause	Professor		38	Prussia
	Harriet	Wife		34	Clerkenwell
	Albert	Son		10	Kensington
	Marie	Daughter		4	Kensington
	Elvena	Daughter		3	Kensington
	Clara	Daughter	3 mon.		Kensington
	Emily Austen	Bra. unm. Scholar		15	Dalston
	Harriett Towns	Dom.		27	Gosport
	Marion Tack	Nurse		18	Scotland

Krause probably the first occupier,
looking for green fields,
open country on the edge of town.
On one side a builder, Scantlebury,
on the other Robinson, vicar of St. Clements.
The solid middle, buying with taste
in the wake of speculation
(70,000 in the borough, 1861 —
by 1881, 165,000).

Movement doesn't stop
as streams are buried
and the crescents spread out in ripples.

> The clerk of No. 2 District, Mr. Parkhouse
> writes in his Valuation Notebook, 1880-81:
> Being converted into shop. E[mpty]
>   pencilled
>   comment

By 1883 the National Stores Provision Co.,
Edward Lee, manager, has premises at 102–106,
the whole row almost, bar the public house and 108.
This continues till 1886, with Krohn & Co., watchmakers
in 108 (later the public library). But 1888 documents
show National Stores, Alfred Drew, Proprietor
at 106 only, with a Butcher, Stapleton at 104
and the National Bakery Company at 102.

Tradespeople breaking through
but permission only for nicer classes of shop —
bread, meat, provisions
for the tide of occupants.

1889: National Stores, Lee & Co., proprietors.
1890: 102 disappears, Stapleton is still in 104, and now
for the first time Cullen Wm. H., Grocer, appears,
business down to the one shop.

A photo from the 1890s has the new Public Library
beside a resplendent 106: *W.H. CULLEN*
                    Grocer Wine Spirit & Beer Merchant
the window piled high with bottles and packets,
a sign on the glass recommending *Fry's Pure Cocoa*,
and an orb-lamp in the doorway.
Above, plants are festooned from iron railings
where a bay window spreads in a triple arch
beneath the second floor balcony,
the whole set firm with a notched cornice.

Today the stucco peels, stone fragments drop
and weeds inhabit rotting woodwork.
Bruno said the forms of deformed animals are beautiful
in heaven. I would place them here.

Rogue Font

20 yards from my door
downstream
the Elgin:
a pint glass
to catch the sound of other voices

name, pedigree, trade
and story
poured at an angle

scraps of heroic
face and type
fitted in a sure elapse

just the grain, just the cut of
that common diet
done special
makes the line

sit up and go

each mouth
it blows
a bag of news
mayn't be sitch a taradiddle

was you, were I
the folk to frot and jag
then what's lost or broke
shall join again
geezers on a ledge

Plumb

That block of flats on the corner, Clare Gardens, used to be a nunnery, and if you was hungry you could knock at the door and the sisters of the poor would give you a handout. The Church sold it out to the council and the price was, I'm not sure, but it could have been over a million pound, maybe two million. The nuns used to go round to all the shopkeepers and beg for food for the poor, but the funny thing about it was, they had a big Rolls Royce and on the side they had a box with a slit in it—a hole to put your money in. At the moment it's a multiracial people here: some are good, some are bad. Things changed when the immigrants came in. See, all these houses, as we know'em, were family houses, and you got the Rachmans moving in, the property speculators. They saw a quick buck and they bought these houses up — maybe for five or six hundred pounds in them days — and they just put a bit of rough furniture and an old cooker in and let'em out at three or four pound a week rent. The people had no recourse whatsoever because there was no rent tribunals or nothink like that: a landlord could get hold of you and sling you out — chuck your belongings in the street — and you couldn't do nothin about it, he was within the law. When Rachman moved into this area he really cleaned up: he took all that property over up in St Stephen's Gardens, and round there. Even today the Government does not know, nor the Police does not know, what property that man owned. No way. He died taking his secrets to the grave. He's not dead yet. You've still got a few people like him, but they keep within the scope of the law — *just* within it. Rachman used to let his property out to prostitutes and what'ave-you, 'cause this was a great area for prostitutes, this was the greatest area in the world for prostitutes. You could go out and pick up a bag anytime you like for a couple of quid. I'm giving you facts: you could buy what you like. There was all little clubs opened up where you could go and drink all day and all night long, and it became suddenly a very rough area. 'Ow can people afford to live here any more? Because it's getting ridiculous now with all the rates and the rats in the property. This used to be a good working-class area, inasmuch that down in Latimer Road and round there—where they've got big blocks of flats—there used to be lots of little industries. You know the manhole covers on the coal 'oles—they made them in Notting 'ill. You can see'em. We had blacksmiths and wheel-makers, and we haven't got nothin now. Who do I blame? The Council, who destroyed them completely. The firms might have only employed two or three people but they gave work to people, inasmuch that they used to say, 'Well, I'll go down to so-and-so.' You take the bridge up the top there, going over the canal—made by Bartle's in Lancaster Road. How bad, how bad? Where Christie lived, at the side of Rillington Place, there's a big chimney. Years ago that was a foundry which made all sorts of things. Then it was turned into a coachworks, which has gone too. There's nothing left here. I've used the Elgin since nineteen-hundred-and-thirty-eight. There's only one man that can beat me, old Fred Porter, who used to stoke the boilers when they was coke burners. The same people don't use that pub—they've died off, or they've vanished, or they've moved away. All these people that use the Elgin today, they're strangers. They might have used it for four years but . . . The Gas works at the top of Ladbroke Grove was destroyed by North Sea Gas. Used to employ a lot o' people—three shifts: six till two, two till ten, ten till six. They had retort houses and everything up there—the OG (oil gas) and the GI system that was the most modern, come from Germany, and you used to make gas out of anything, out of wood. It's a massive piece of ground up there and it's derelict now. Christie used to be a foreman or a doorman at a cinema in Lancaster road called The Royalty—that spare bit of ground where there's nothing at the moment. He would pick up prostitutes at Jock's Cafe, which was on the corner, and take them to 10

Rillington Place. The rest of that is history: you can read that in any book, what he used to do to them. He was accused of killing them first and having sexual intercourse with them when they was dead. I lived at number 16, just a few doors away. My little girl was born there. But they changed the name from Rillington Place to Ruston Close, because there was too many tourists coming over and causing aggravation to the tenants. They took that name from the road opposite, Ruston Mews, which also follows the line o'the railway. Even Ruston Close has gone now. Modern flats, modern houses, are there now. The oven, the forge, has all gone. Christie was a very meek and mild man. He often used to go in Bill's Cafe on the corner of Rillington Place. Nobody suspected him, because the first person he killed was Timmy Evans' wife — and baby. He gave them an abortion and she died and he killed the baby and he buried it. Even the police in their fuckin stupidity, they found the bodies there with bones and everything, and they crucified the wrong man. Because Timmy Evans was a bit — you know, he wasn't altogether there. He worked as a driver for a furniture removal business in Latimer Road at the time, but he was a bit mental — he didn't have his faculties all about him. If it had been a man with a bit of intelligence the Old Bill would have come unstuck, but they crucified him because he was stupid. He went down. They believed Christie because he had been a special constable during the war. Anyway, eventually Christie was married to a German woman — I can't remember whether he killed his wife before Timmy Evans' wife and baby or whether he killed her afterwards — but he killed his wife and he told everybody she'd gone back to Germany. Then he had to get out of his house for some reason — I don't know whether he owed rent or wanted to go — and the next tenant was a coloured bloke name of Mr Brown, who wanted to do some decorations and that. If you know the houses in Rillington Place like I know'em, it was very easy to hide bodies. They was like doll houses, very narrow, but there was all these chinks and crannies. The floorboards, the joists from the bottom of the floor, was a couple of feet deep. They was slung up in the industrial revolution — you could hide bodies there unbelievable and get away with it. And he sold his house or the owner let it out, and Mr Brown took over, started tapping the walls, tearing the paper away. Only to discover this alcove. At the top of the road there was Andrews Garage — still there today — and lo and behold he went flying up to the garage to ring the police, and then the bubble burst. They came down and they found all these bodies. But previous to that they found bones in the garden that belonged to his wife and they thought they was animal bones. Now 'ow can you possibly associate an animal bone with a human bone? But the Old Bill did. Said they're animal bones and he fobbed them off. After the bubble burst they found out more and more and more. He had hooks and he used to hang'em up by the bra. He killed more prostitutes than enough. Rillington, Ruston, somebody told me they're Yorkshire names and Christie was born up there. Rill, I think, means a little stream — you've got big and small streams in Notting 'ill. The river comes down from Westbourne Park Road here, part of the Westbourne. It runs under the bank and sweeps round by Ladbroke Grove and it goes under the block of flats which we know as Lancaster Court. There's a massive well, four foot square in the basement — you can go and see it if you get permission from the owner. Years ago they used to pump the water out. I think they just made it part of the drainage system. If you go to the Jewish school, which has closed down, you'll find another well which still keeps coming up and it's beautiful pure water. Then you've got the river Worm which comes down from Wormwood Scrubs, and years ago you had a racecourse here. The Hippodrome used to run from the Potteries — Pottery Lane it's still there — right round by Holland Park Avenue and up towards the Scrubs. If you go to number 20 Lansdowne Crescent you can see one of the original posts. St John's Church, at the top of the 'ill, was the grandstand — before any church was there. As well as the industry, a lot of farm work used to go on here. Campden was a village years ago and Portobello Road was a cart track which went up to Admiral Vernon's farm. Before I was a twinkle in the old man's eye. But I know a lot about Notting 'ill and I've seen many changes. This street has a crater at the end, blocking it off. Yes, I can never understand why they done that, because there used to be two streets branched off, Talbot Grove and Camelford Road, and in the middle there was a big pub belonged to Courages which they called The Ladbroke. It was a massive place and they pulled it down and built that school. But they went down so deep when they was building. The bomb dropped a way back. If you look at Ladbroke Crescent you've got 1-8, and there's 9, 10, 11 and 12, I think, or 9, 10 and 11 are missing. You have a little block of flats there, which is where the bomb dropped. It shook all these houses. But the Ladbroke was never bombed: that's not a bomb crater, that was dug out by man, because I watched it being done. That wasn't done by Hitler because I don't think he was big enough to knock the Ladbroke down anyway. The pubs. We used to have a chap come in with a bag of rats and for a shilling he would bite their heads off — alive, urgh! Nobody really took to him. We had characters come round and chew beer glasses — anything to get a living. I don't know how they dunnit. There was sword-swallowers as well. We had all sorts of people. But you could keep a family on a lot cheaper than you could today. They was hard days but they weren't bad days. In Elgin Mews, opposite, under the arch, they housed all the coaches and the horses. This was a very select area. You got lords and ladies living in Westbourne Park Road. Lord Elgin was a big man round here, like Lord Holland. He used to go and dig up all these old graves in Egypt, and the pub was named after him. Most of this property belonged to him. He had a big influence in the area. I've only listened to what old people tell me. You've got to take this handed down from word to mouth. There was stables too in Vernon Yard, which is now a classy place: moneyed people moved in. Those stables belonged to Humphreys, the removal firm. Another company, Davies, had coaches used to run out the Portobello Road. You could go round to these places and they'd give you a day's work. Used to be a blacksmith's would shoe horses for a couple of shillings a shoe. They would make the shoe and fit it on. Top wack. That was a lot of money in them days. You go in the pub and buy a pint of beer or a packet of woodbines for fourpence. You could get drunk on two bob. Now can't get drunk on ten pound. They don't make beer like they used to in them days. I mainly drank Mainline then. Guinness was a good drink, and Burton was too. Mainline was a Taylor Walker's drink, strangely enough, a genuine one, not what you get today under the same name. They're bringing the old brands back but not the beer. When that came out it was a good strong ale. I'm going back forty years now. In them days beer was brewed in wooden barrels and they had quarry slates inside. Roofing slates to us. I can't explain it but I saw how they did it at the Watney's brewery in Pimlico. Now it's stainless steel and all that rubbish, and the beer's not the same. Six pints of beer these days and you've had enough. All these pubs round here were Taylor Walker's then, including the KPH. Beer, weather, that's what you remember. When I was a boy we couldn't sleep in the house during the summer. Too hot. The beds were crawling with bugs. So we would sit out on the doorstep. Adventures, roughing it a bit, got you ready for responsibility. After leaving school at fourteen, I went to serve an apprenticeship as a plumber and we worked in lead—for which we got a pint of milk a day by law, like painters and printers. Any man that had anything to do with lead. It came in a big tube and you had to make the pipes your own length. You had to dress it and sweat it and everything. No call for it today. It's all pretty made up now. Every man took a pride in his craft and if you didn't do your job properly your master would give you a wallop. It took five years to train—working round Kensal Rise, all over the place. It was hard: lead is bloody heavy stuff. It was dirty: you used plumber's black, made of carbon and glue, before soldering. 'Blue'. It was fiddly: you needed a rasp, a shavehook, an auger, tallow, moleskins. Still got the gear. They're only fitters now— they just fit pipes together and that's all there is to it. But we knew how to live it up. There was music halls and wrestling in Edgware Road and the Electric Cinema in Portobello Road. The bug'ole, as we called it, the first of its kind, all lit up by gaslight. It cost a couple of coppers to get in there. All sorts of entertainment we used to make: cards, dominoes, draughts. We would sit up till two o'clock in the morning and listen to the radio. Even though America was 3,000 miles away, we used to get it on the old battery set with accumulators. One of 'em would run down half way through a big fight from America and the old man used to do his nut. On public holidays you would load up a coach with booze and all go down to Brighton or Clacton, bring back rock, winkles and prawns. Health? Well, let's put it this way: the only people I know dying of cancer in them days was old people—over seventy. Now you get kids of five, six, seven dying of it. You can draw your own conclusions. Pressure. And I don't think the food is as good as it used to be. Everything is forced. The potatoes are forced with arsenic, forced through the ground. Everything is refrigerated now and no animal or human manure is used for growing. Everybody in them days made their own bread—you never got it from no factory. Every baker made his own bread. You buy a loaf now, leave it three days, and it goes mildewy.

Footnote

To start with the water
which modern maps don't give you:
by the Worm he means Counter's Creek,
the boundary rivulet coming down
west of Barlby Road and this whole area,
from Wormwood Scrubs or Wormholt Wood Common,
once called Bridge Creek, then Billingwell Ditch,
and described in the deed of 1599 as the *Common Sewer*,
a stream now covered in and sewerized, official,
though it still runs four miles
and discharges itself into the Thames at Chelsea Creek.
That you can see: disheartened marguerite daisies
and thistles growing beside green slime.

Today, having walked, and seen,
and gone back to the charts,
I find he's right too about the standing water
or streams which run
between the Westbourne and Counter's Creek —
viz. on John Wyld's map, 1833, a tributary brook
starting close to Portobello Farm
and running through marshy ground
at the foot of the north slope of St. John's Hill
to join the Creek by Latimer road,
just across from the Potteries.
On Wyld's 1850 map, after the railway,
this water has disappeared
underground.

Barton, in *Lost Rivers*, has this
stopping short of Ladbroke Grove
but plans of the Hippodrome, 1837 & 1841,
show that enclosure bounded on the north
by a line between Lancaster Road and Cornwall
(or Westbourne Park) Road, apparently
along the course of the brook from Portobello Farm.

Which confirms this — library, pub, and bank —
as the central point, hereabouts.
Hippodrome and Potteries the two ends of life:

the former 'projected' by Mr. John Whyte
who took a twenty-one year lease of 140 acres
from Ladbroke in August 1836
to lay out courses for steeplechasing and flat-racing,
a grand scheme by which spectators
could view the races from start to finish
as riders galloped round the knoll.
An enterprise open to the fertilization
of many sources of profit
but which obstructed the footpath
from Kensington to Kensal Green and Willesden —
whence invasion of the grounds and court cases.
After the course had been diverted north-west,
into a bulb shape, and rough people excluded,
a *brilliant & immense assembly* enjoyed the sport,
but it still did not pay and the gates were closed.
So to the building of the '40s and '50s,
crescents and gardens, which echoed Whyte's dream
(*inner space* returning, says Mumford).

Beside that, almost, the Potteries or Piggeries
lying at the foot of the hill and bypassed
by railway arches, the low clay pockmarked
by excavations filled with stagnant water —
like 'the Ocean', one sheet an acre wide.
A primæval swamp blossoming in broken bottles,
pots and pans, the well-water black as chimney-brick.
A west-end *Avernus* (1893), every other child
dead by the age of one.

Reason for not living back then,
get air and water to build that dream.
Rooting for this in the back row of the Electric
swigging a litre of Valpolicella
and swaying, my other arm round her
to keep the show from closing.

Dreads and Drolls

23 Clarendon Road, 1883.
A room at the top, a very small room,
not even a monastic cell.
A bed, a washstand, small table, one chair,
no fireplace.
A gas-jet, meter shut off at midnight,
a kettle and spirit-lamp.
Carriage candles for reading —
Burton, Homer,
Don Quixote, Hargrave Jennings
on the Rosicrucians.
Black wrack of pipe smoke
over yellow gorse.
A loaf of bread, canister of green tea
in the corner.
A box of possessions, sparse
on the landing.
Hung lengthwise, a step-ladder
in case of fire.
Between rungs, a library of sorts.

Tramp the road north
in search of green.
Loaf, stroll through a cat's-cradle
of blocks, across the canal
and round to a walled, grass desert
of shattered marble pillars,
granite urns.

```
        free from
tight               weather
        the heart
back                sinks
    to thicket
```

Out of this maze by obscure paths
with a gusty, restless wind

over the moonbridge, quivering iron
to smug villas, a last piano note
alive as coals
behind close-drawn curtains.

Who is that girl arms jerked up
frantic wires pulling
to beckon/run
in leafy shadow squares

what   this
   is   is
     home, what

      hill
      of
      dreams

Horizon vague in purple mist
to first sun and duty,
the hum and jangle of trams

up by taller elms and planes
for paper and ink
from Murley's, celestial stationer

   to plot out a book
in the carpet, design faded
   to build a mosaic
    memory and echo
     of music
   dark beneath sense
on a ruled white sheet

Sopho-spagirical realms of congyration
where neumes are story and person,
no foregone ethic to dash effect

dig and burrow

to make of these avenues of lamps
    this starry labyrinth
        Baghdad, Sion
           the city of the cup
        gold never found
    but *rarities*
rich underneath

So to come through the terror
dry rotted to the cock-loft
that aumbry which may crack and thunder
in a moment, and furnish tales
to the eighth day

journeys, histories
from a throbbing head
and a Viaduct pen

matter everywhere present
in gaps and silence

a half-glance in the cave of Rabelais—
hard words to take or treat

bou bou   brededin, brededack
cushotten   godderlich
jadish   laycod
nimming   omee of the carser
nunty munjare   parastata
soritick   stymphalid
whirreted   whinyard

cast by rhizotome
they go
tuberous on night watch
under the gas-jet

Nuttyngwood (knotting)
to Caerleon-on-Uske, a framed jest

for bosky relation
now the scene breathes
by back travel

such toil to prod and poke
    walls and trees
a world drawn in marks
    put aside

Say you know but who
    is the other
    that hides

Rule of Mouth

for Jeff Nuttall, 8.9.80

if you tape
       record
   concerts you have
          to hold
    your body   rigid
not even drink beer
can't clap   in case
the sound   dis torts

            scald

wall   field

       flesh

only sure   catches
what leaps   from
glass some fleeting
    wolverine   like
          trr-add
   gone harmolodic

        poets are
cornet-players

bright in forgotten folds

Frame Slip

Driving north out of London
after a night of love,
a green light up Chamberlayne
Sidmouth a rush of cherry blossom,
I follow the radio curves—
Jean-Marie Leclair—
think I'll head east for the coast
today. Flute Strings & Continuo
can't force me into corridors
hooks on either wall

Work tore the top
off my briefcase

Babylonian Room

There's nothing to do, nowhere to go and no one to visit.
Don't stay overnight in town—brothers kill brothers here.
If you eat at Leon's Café, don't be fooled by the way
folks seem friendly at first—
they're just edging in for a clearer shot.
Try to look like other people in Westgate:
Carry a .45 automatic, paint your face grey,
cough a lot and never smile unless someone dies.

I'll burn you with gaudy bars, stub out your longing,
and drive high into the mountains.
I'll spit words that'll bust your vision,
break your glass and bury bedsprings
so none of those words in the dictionary survive.

The role of this station in peacetime
is to prepare for war
and don't you forget it. Perfumed talk looping over

———————————

The line, if you could only see, you've been fooled
and cheated out of the knowledge of your condition:
That red cleft is to get you back, to gasp for air,
a tent or wattled hut where you can dig yourself in.

My face covers your face like a mother.
I'll place you like a jewel between my breasts,
during the night I'll give you covering,
during the day I'll clothe you.
Don't be afraid to use this earth-bed.
I walked in juddering seams, stripped off in each precinct
a piece of myself: the great crown from my head,
pendants from my ears, the necklace from my throat,
gems from my breast, my girdle adorned with birthstones,
the bracelets from my hands and feet,
and finally the cloth which covered my readiness.
From this I walked out free, understanding who I am.

QUEEN ON THAT COUCH, A BANQUET DELIGHTING THE HEART. ISHTAR

Script Rip

Cutting through ultimate spinach —
freak equipment, light and stage stock

    zap, the dinosaurs are gone
    under their own weight
    eyes down, cameras rolling

Back to the gear you need:
bass, drums & rhythm,
maybe a shot of tenor sax

three-finger chords
cause you gotta hear the sweat

    pumping vocal
    sliced with tremolo
    amps clipped by the law

Try to go past always
the programme finish
with enemy stutter — am am
amber dawn finding a shape
in sharded riffs and looping bass,
no money and no time for tomorrow

phrase over plot, she's the one
strides a crystal tip

    streaks in your hair,
    undertaker paint,
    stretch & shine of leather, silk
    make a city of words
    (there is no eye: only
    a series of mouths)

Can't explain, it was just there
and the line came out

you shot your sperm into me
but never set me free

All these lads screaming for knickers
might throb might burn
a picture to stake

now on the whirl she mikes
a reply, Fishnet is flesh, jo gob
(can't get into everybody's head)

they're not love songs
but honest songs,
mona lisa, couldn't
couldn't please her

There are no islands left
for us to play,
the Rock Garden or Dingwalls
is where the Photos
come alive

L'Inverno

Fourth place after the hunt
and also the first   violin winds
as I follow my father
through fields unmarked at sight
by toil or trade

we haul out the cases of wine,
he savouring each shape and weight,
I pile the barrow high
with cheer

Lafite-Rothschild '49
Chateau Latour '54
a vintage port almost
forgotten

ripeness trapped for a gentleman's
penury   to stir the blood   in a Russian
night   Others are skating
caught in drifts   we move
together   attuned   to the grey
sky and vault of ice

The Gascon Scarlet is there
lopped three years ago
the Blenheim stands gaunt
ten apples only now
but the King of the Pippins
yields store for a family
still

a hammock hung between boughs
gnarled   mother's white dress in the shade
her form outstretched, dignified
as one of Chekhov's women

Pizzicato bites the season
back   the birdbath
an uneven cone

The labels wiped clean we know
our separate memories

The hut by the stream where I stood guard
while my sister kissed my best friend
the water we were forbidden to cross
because a baby drowned
the sand my other sister ate
when it was left for play

we trudge back in a fugal
passage   the house   smaller
in adulthood   breathes   frozen
pincered heavy

Three windows mark a space
at the top where I stayed
with an older woman
(the neighbours never talked)

Brave the slipway boy
your sisters did it easily

I couldn't till I was away
whisky in a brown paper bag
gave myself to a stranger

You turned the lights out
one by one when you
were in need of work

and I   lost in the study
of happiness   gave you
no strength or beauty

The Tricolore/the white cockade
a single strain for two
forces   as Lili Marleen
in the trance of war

incense smoke over D-Day speed
a freakish point to meet

We share a landscape now
we live under different roofs
it's taken thirty winters
to find this territory

Yet still I don't take my girlfriend
home because she's seventeen
and would talk about bombs in Bologna

Play-bill

Prolonged a week in the height of summer
I counsel you come to the bearded heart
for history re-set in sartorial cut-up —
a half-moon of flesh as she bends
to sip bubbly from a slipper, his
upturned pinstripe feel.

It's standing room only on Union Street:
they seem to behave much better
if their roots are crushed together
and they have to fight for their lives.

Drink in all opportunities,
just jobs, your car, TV and house
when the old myths don't work:
even the yoghurts have been stabbed
and spilled everywhere,
a solstice over trenches and razor wire.

End-of-empire evasions
an adrenalin of greed
when the latest is the only truth
set in ELEPHANT type
and you're writing for those twenty readers
between the starched line and the cheap gag.

Work a lime for a month, super for a fortnight
to get a single day on the boards
and then wait for tragedians
to slide from the circle
like a hundred peacocks
returning.

An ink man is a prince
in borstalled imagination
greased with running patter:
let's close this joint or hold it
a cigarette against a silver balloon
hung from a fish-tail cadillac.

Southam Street

1985–1986

I

PRESLEY IS MAD/I love elvis
ELVIS IS/D Cox/A Pelvis
JW/The King/THE POX
SANDRA MILLS IS
ELVIS YOU ARE THE ONE
YVONNE I LOVE YOU
I'm Blue today

scratched and proud
the iron bridge
by the Earl of Warwick
speaks mean
its railway dreams

black and white
Fifties instant
of winter

a sheet of glamour and chores
contacting into a chunky casbah

the Ted who turns, suddenly operatic,
his long jacket and mirror shoes
an invitation to be on

the blonde eight-year-old
perched on the handlebar
who rides a tricycle backwards

the four women linking arms
who gaze beneath scarf and grips
with a hard, still generous alertness

the brylcreem boy
who measures an adult's wheel
against a child's bike
while his sister holds a toddler
in the saddle

the goalposts drawn on the wall
to catch shadows

the casual walking and talking
that is foregrounded
by braces of assertion.

II

Is this more than a museum
my eyes seem to tread,
of frills dispersed
by a locomotive
in the spine

the final business
a boot repairer
at number 92,
a game of poker
on the steps

spiv and spade parings
hot after ferreting,
a neighbourhood job

What you done then,
the groceries c'n wait—
Mae shuffles in slippers
as the Wolseley arrives

a tremor from the tracks
to the canal

closed basements
of rheumatism and consumption,
bottle glass scattered
like diamonds in the asphalt

a black terrier limps
toward a shock of children,
the girls in short socks
swinging from a street lamp
or pressed in a handstand
against corrugated sheets
while the boys shout
'Ropem and Chokem'
or 'Catch a falling sputnik':

games in the chalk circle
and waiting for thruppence
an infectious soccer urgency
between the peeling terraces
of another century

the gas-works at the north end
and the glistening kerbstone edge
aligning each event.

III

CLASS WAR/Mandy I love you
IF VOTING MADE ANY DIFFERENCE
THEY'D ABOLISH IT/Boy is a junkie
AMERICA THE GREAT DEVIL/Go home
you sod/Sniff le sex test
THIS IS NOT A LOVE SONG
Elvis Costello no's it/COLOUR
BY NUMBERS

with a long diesel choke
the 'Repulse' heads out
beyond Portobello Junction
aching for tunnels
and the west

'Sowtham Street'
says the red-faced gorger
outside the Earl (differing
from the librarian's 'Suthem'),

yes it used to run
one long street
from the bottom there
up to the bend
into Southern Row
and this was the middle,
the bridge

RAILWAY houses
they was originally,
backed up against the railway
with railway people living there
I think

more deaths than anywhere,
it was poky
but I tell you
it was a community

now there's just
these fifty yards

the Council mowed everything down
when they did their New Town scheme

I'm not complaining, mind,
I've got my own place—
one family one place
that's what you get
with the modern.

IV

You could buy a pennyworth of pickles
from the corner shop—
that would be a little on top
or it would keep you going

Saturday night was the big blow-out
when the fellas used to come home
rollin and singing

hair was on the ground and blood
but you was mates again afterwards

Black Harry: the kids would wait
to touch him when he came out
because they thought he was lucky

you didn't have a bath,
there might just be a gas ring
on the landing

but there was grapes and fruit
carved at the sides of the fireplaces

you never had nothing
but you had everything
because you had your friends

you had the streets
because there were none of them
comforts inside, no television

you grew a character
of your own.

V

A photograph of the Robin Hood
and Little John, October 1967 —
a bulky round-cornered pub
at the south-eastern end
by the junction
with Kensal Road

its stately windows agape,
doors boarded, a broken Victorian,
the name and brewery erased
even before demolition

the road designated
'Play Street'.

VI

Pregnancies, washing & the DHSS:
Trellick Tower, with thirty floors
stands up a concrete giant,
a nucleated village
or Druid inferno

the lift section, with ten bridges,
four funnels and slits like a castle,
is called 'The Psychiatric Wing'
because when the lifts break down
you don't want to come out

the best view of London,
she said

a man spits with vehemence,
a boy drags a scaffolding pole
into the sunken playground

which already boasts
a log frame, swings
and fixed red bars

the breeze block walls
are a honeycomb
blackened in fifteen years

'Billy Butler' painted cheerfully
in white, a reassertion

as the pigeons swoop from neat boxes
and polychrome panels
to gut stale loaves
stuffed into a lorry-size
refuse drum.

VII

Space there is and colour
and tolerable health
marked by what persists
in parallel:

J. Wilmot (Curtain Makers),
Southern Row,
four fireplaces
on an outside wall
like Moloch's eyes

a passage to the Grove
with steps, railings and two metal posts,
'KP 1867' set into the brickwork,
'Ancient Lights' on the cellar door.

VIII

I am a street/survivals and mutations
baby-ridden and eager,
I am a plot on soapsuds island—
market of the land,
I am a pocket of laughter
while the smokes go round,
I am the skirt who walks out at night
mutely trailing my drainpipe lad,
I am the tinderbox, black hair
streaked with silver

has you twist to the tone
of a pink bakelite radio
unexpectedly cruising
as keys, the keys
are thrown down.

Note

Southam Street was developed in the 1860s and 1870s and figures as a depressed area in Booth's survey of 1902. Its location was unpropitious: a narrow piece of ground between the Great Western Railway and the Grand Junction Canal. Severe overcrowding led to its having the highest rate of infectious diseases in Kensington. In the 1950s the street was known as the worst slum in the borough: a graphic account can be found in the autobiography of Michael X (Malick). At the same time (1956–61), Roger Mayne was taking photographs which have become a vivid testament to the life of the area. A large selection was published in the magazine *Uppercase* (1961) and this forms the basis of *The Street Photographs of Roger Mayne* (Victoria and Albert Museum, 1986).

In his original introduction Mayne wrote:

> I photograph Southam Street because it is beautiful and because the people have great vitality, especially the children. This I think reflects a positive way of life; at the moment the planners are not sufficiently awake to the qualities of these streets which ultimately will have to go.

The street was demolished in 1968–69 as part of a comprehensive redevelopment and the old layout is impossible to visualize without the aid of maps. Trellick Tower, which stands adjacent to Portobello (or Golborne Road) bridge, was formerly the tallest residential building in England. It was designed by Ernő Goldfinger in 1972.

Uncollected

1985

Chipscore for Love (or, the Mediated Muse)

arm in apposite arch
inaidible inaurate
inark inaunter
inactuate in-
and-in inasmuch
inamorata inborn
inbring inboard
initinitselfinburst
inbyeincaincandesce
incantareincalescent
incapsulateincarnadine
incenseincentreincessant
inchaseinchoateincident
incipientinclaspincline
inclipincludeincorporate
increaseincrescentincubate
incurrentincurveincusindia
indagateindartindefinable
indewindexindigoindicia
inditeindoorindraft
indrawnindrench
indubitable
induce induct indue
    indulge   indwell
inebriate   ineffable
ineluctable   inerasable
inessive   inestimable
in excelsis inexhausted
in extenso   inextinguishable
infall   infant   infare
     infelt   infilling
   infinite inflammable
        inflate
inflorescence   inflow
infoldinform
           infrastructure
          infuse

                    ingan   ingate
                          ingathering
                       ingenerate
                    ingest
ingrainingressingrooveinguinal
inhabitinhaleinhaustinhere
inhoopinjellyinjointinjun
inlet in limine inlock
in media res inn inmost
innervateinorbinordinate
inositol   inphase
in puris naturalibus
inquiline inquire
insalivate inship

                                                        insooth
                                                        insphere
                                                        inspirit
                                                        instar
                                                        instauration
                                                        instigate
                                                        instinct

                    INTAGLIO

             integer

    intelsat

             intenerate   interbedded

    intercellular   interchange

             intercontinental   intercrural

INTERFACE INTERFOLD INTERFUSE INTERGALACTIC INTERLACE INTERPLAY INTERTANGLE   INTERVEIN

                                                                                        INTERVOLVE

INTIMATE
INTIME
INTINCTION
IN TOTO
INTRAMERCURIAL
INTRINSIC

inwit inwith inwrap
in vino veritas
inyala
inverness

introjection
intuition
inundate   in   in   in   in   in   in   invent

forkristin   *gavinladbrokegrove*   25.3.85

from **Strip Signals**

1985-1986

Now an unforgetting is taking place. The mind picking its way through parallel universes: a weird time in which we are alive, travelling anywhere we want. There are rooms with star-demons, the whole sky on a dial. A register to call in traces. Run the tape back in my head, trying to write *King Lear* in an age of domestic realism. Can't dream the same dreams when you're thirty-six that you did when you were twenty-four, but you can still dream something. A twelve-foot ladder turns into Heartbreak Hotel.

Acquired stock electronically configured, a generating station, night and day a furious courier, a lottery of upstart authority with sweat appraisal. The city's golden boy, doubling values in an information stream as people with carrier bags over their heads yell at traffic. A jobber's notebook filled with strange characters: Mzazo Ozlacim, Ozazm Micalzo. 30 calls yet to come. Cross-match, convert to yield. By suppression or removal these fragments will speak, marble, agate under dust. Wake Cleopatra to force out spoil, outperform the index. Shush-ort hedge bet placed ticktack. A toolbox of derivatives, solids thinner than air with the glint of arrival. Bang on target, just hang in to force-connect and quit. Hide any strong seething over terms or partner pitch.

Oh the curse of conjuration: a sentence in the scroll dimly lit, half-rehearsed and liable to slip, leaving a blank then a bloodshot screen. The sole gate, the link of links, won't work or, worse, brings a hostile spirit, serves a revolute deal. Wh-wha-what you bargain for and what you get. Compress weariness, a load dispatcher, shadow of a brain, life-rentrix. Ensnared urgency mechanism. He could not lie with her, wedged between tenses, raw with the edge of repetition. Gaze and glance, a hazard of different objects. Allure, alloro, alloy. A smile, powder-driven, shivers back. The only reason people want to buy clothes is to get laid. Someone else will perform.

[. . .]

Tied to a wheel which turns perpetually, she is sometimes rising and sometimes falling. Who would not take his chance and see her mirrored, giddy with longing, a play of hearts in a scented theatre? Forty impressions of a façade with no earth and sky: hope, a capacious sieve, spinning off into her final act. River sand and gold to make ruby glass, coronal, an effect that has never been matched. Forty layers of flashing. The gem at the heart of colour.

He held a bunch of violets in the cathedral close. It was the first time and he was swelled with pride. This was her boudoir and he was a stranger. Would she come? He was afraid of being observed. Light danced on the cobbles. A rustle of silk and he was swept inside. By the still figures, a chorale heard in the pedal, he felt her tottering virtue. Under arches and panels music echoes on white stones in ribbons of blue. As if untried, they pace the holy forest.

Grim god triumphant/a fog in the head. Knowledge and improvement, the books of which we carry printed in our souls. Do thou now learn to order thy materials. Halting syllables pressed into a schoolboy orator's circuit: a traumatic entry into language. A collection never to be dispersed. He sat round a table with upright chairs. 'I feel full' the forbidden phrase. A summons, but the past is contested ground. The sun passes out of his pavilion, draws a verse on the cloth laid out. Air of wilfulness. Shimmer to talk through long afternoon. Champagne runs over the rim of her glass, the whence of desire. A delicate repose is allotted, then the hand removes any front. She spills herself out of herself into everything about her. A departure from the text. Done with a tongue she doesn't recognize.

from **Elizabethan Overhang**

1987–1988

Make-Up

Sling me the run-again please
to not answer in poem poems.
If I could word it through the prism
so the text of ourselves is the text
of an eye beyond, if I could hold
the ebony log straight as it's
squashed into two dimensions,
if I could ease the half-shell
into seas on the lee of engagement,
I would put off the accretion
of legend and love, for these
are sounds forced into a box
to elude the prevailing code
of thinned-out universe terms.

Long Take

What harvest do you find in winter,
down pressed at twice fourteen
with torches of memory — the hall
where you loosed your dress
as boys hardly knew you, pillars
from which your fluxile eyes
said never again the waggoner's scorch
and lilies dispersed from the lap.

A fervent kisser you are despite
one get-out clause in the tenth line,
and climbing from the crannied furnace
you overgo in restless twists
such vows as forbid this least
interpenetrating syntax.

Texarkana

Carries, the red back book
bolder than hearsay. Finger
my leaves, euphonic, ragging
time rebellious and not quite
home against the strong plod
of intention, to turn dead
metaphors into river dancing,
slow on heat's tenderloin verge.

Not closed in hiemal retreat
these shines are bobbing
soft-loud (something like
to unravel and reunite).
Never apologise, she says —
I wear her scent all day.

Idea's Mirror

Set me, you do, singing on as chords
disappear into silence, so Elizian reaches
design to be unstudied, should they be
long mortalized by skin-magic.
I pinned an anchor to your silver scarf:
now the second post brings a card
saying 'I feel good and not so scared'
with 'love' shoved between the lines.

Nights ago you wrote, 'Why ask for a key
when you have had it all the time?'
I wished and these worlds slid together,
my dear meaning lips and limbs.
And the woman you are paragons all forms
that are intimated after or before.

Firstborn

Out at the edge of speech years pass
clingy across distances, what was half-mapped
and nervously handled, to bear proudly
the undone measure of imperial hopes,
home at the breast and never wanting
to stop, in a left-hand relation
substantive, an eye over time's shoulder
ready to be supplanted.
                              Go walking,
an emigrant in firmamental history,
cry cry cry and smile in an after-strife
that opens roses, to climb and model
terraces on the site of buried intention:
sunwise we illumine — fearing and feared
for the visage we suggest of digging paradise.

Delayed Release

Who are we, meeting ourselves going back
in the Chelsea Drugstore, blame put squarely
on the me experiment, the communal lie
by which free-floating figures were promised.
Sold out, they say, or crushed in taste,
the seed won't deliver — its consummation
encycled to waste — for all the world
like a private number dialled in nostalgia.
But everybody sings, everybody writes
making it outside high industry
as the official tab runs down care
and won't enter imagine's intensity.
Still waves abound to cross a second boom:
what's played out early is no threat to the womb.

Tundale

And now we are called to account, in a failure
of memory, the drumbeat making bad blood
emerge from a dance-hall decade of abandon,
as if the way we were was some superior sap.
Hold up the mirror and we are monsters
slithering across each other's loins,
our gossamer wings bogged in dishonour
while the magistrate of games looks on.
Should we creep out of these flower peelings,
abbreviate this prancing round the pool,
when each strawberry in smell and taste
calls up a prospect of antibodies?
It is a park of altered habits, no reason
to deny what we gained in the fairest season.

One is Two

Not all the words which shore belief
can say what it is that pulls us
tidelong from one state to another —
to roll and push and burst
then drift back over sand ridges,
to argue, hurt and flip out
in bottle tremors that translate
as deep nerve-fire glows.
Granted, this is no passport
into the years, nor to any fastland
beyond the white horse, maybe
we're no faultier than those
whose emblem is a dry rise
set firm in symbiotic guise.

Phyletic

Blood on her T-shirt marks the difference
between night and morning, a delicate print
from the shoulder, softer than soft,
hinting at how more than sips were taken
when these Ur-selves escaped, by parachute
jumps from the bar, by a traffic cone
on his head, streaking to translate
Mozart on a ghetto-blaster in Walpole Park.

'Fickle sickle,' she said, looking up
as the cracked sole of her pointed boot
wrote a signature on heaven's floor.
But her eyes, lightly furrowed in laughter,
disclosed that our names (under star-logic)
make a puzzle of interlocking syllables.

In and Out Of

Five notes on a flute and the film slips back:
I am there with you — a dial in the garden,
somewhere without waiting, like habit
not duty, as ripples come and go
in a silent pool. Your mouth floats yeses
of undenomination, your eyes lift a longness
into smiling, your hair smooths elision
with April highlights in a round of years.
Just when we breathe, between the toc and tic
an old reproach grabs us: we are thrown
by the thought of a rod on a silk cord,
an anchor, dead beat or cylinder escapement,
and we are jigged into hand over hand marching
in a wrung haste to nowhere.

Textural

In the first September of our seeing
I knew that we would redraw the story,
our knees touching under the table,
and so did you, you say, get an inkling
of that claret flush on the plateau
of shared arrival. You blushed
over your name, or was it the likelihood
of filling lines in a dateless book.
Shyly, you caught my gaze, led me slowly
into December, with parkland kisses
over the gear-shift and a perfumed pillow
on the spare bed from which I stole
to yours. There we wrote a hook
made all the song seem whole.

Transfer

Tracing these characters on the pane
I see your sexy hand, feel
parts of love, over and over,
was it night-nurse, whisky or your daytime self
came intimate, across a distance
in curves and strokes, to colour
my bleached hours, relimb
the abstract moment, at seventeen
on a one-way street
whose language will not deign
to replay the neural conjunction,
the touch that makes us kin,
so the surface will not take
anything more than a matchstick man
with a stuck-on nose.

Obsession

I thought I was hearing you see me
seeing you, such alteration being
unreason's reason, a crystal tone
Englishing the displaced body
of foreign syllables, so no voice chip
could ever repeat the sheer L
our chorus climbed, that light
in the can't which makes all go.

With your one-coin calls at three a.m.
and one-person packets from the corner shop,
you pass and repass the round o's
of will you still love me — tomorrow.
And those lady's-traces ring clear
as tracks on a lost acetate.

Less and More

Moved like a man, she let me be that
coming on out the other side of neutral
after role reversal, when considerate becomes
not easily prized spaghetti twists,
cooked and gone cold in a hyperbaton
of this ought we to manifest —
the slash in the circle that forbids
winding up to a double negative.
Nor nothing is indubitable
if we're vascular, crystalline and moony.
I did not waver, I was one voice
uplifted from a leased time-slot
cancelling skidmarks on a rusty overhang
as also a jutting memoried splendour.

Psychotronic

Don't for god's sake fall in love
with a poet, he'll make you
mirror-keen as the lost
language of petticoat schemes,
he'll hang far off in another
plantation while he's sucking
all grace out of you. And if
you seek with one caesura
to slow his tread
through the eight and six,
you'll find there's a wolfgirl
wants to be scratched and bitten
in a couplet with no seams
that connects with his dreams.

Vermilion

There, where her touch was felt
only iron endures, a dead letter-box
on the ridgeway that others run
seeming to scorch slogans
from its otherly-pointed rim.
They are giving their money a workout
so you power up to eighteen per cent.
You reinvent yourself for the occasion
making the same mistakes more slowly.
In strange arms, in knotted sleep
her raven hair and rosy skin
are airs built on a butcher's victory.
No wine-flame or stiletto-fling
can shift the last report.

from **Tilting Square**

1988–1991

Parnassus

Miles out in the black or void you'd think
we're blissed with disturbance, careening
then storm-checked as our letters are etched
by a spear of longing. The picture livens,
accurate in fragments: a mass of swans
is splayed before three human figures
who try to dance before a suspended wall.
Never say never plays the tune, half-aiming
at a marbled future, but most eyes which choose
are fuelled by a vinegar urgency
so the oldest charm is hardly recognized
in a message-hungry network, stopless
from its need to nail the right soulful face
silent or as good as after the prize is won.

Business and Origin

A pleasant reach that must be
for the gems and blossom
those in other walks observe, musing
on the next casual sunset, loosened
from duty to anything but words
when the trick is got through hoops
and wire, as limbs are wrenched
and the brain is squeezed, numb
then dizzy with an urge to bear:
carbon from a bladelike pressure,
black blood traced along decreasing
flesh, to bring life into blank
apartments, a mess of beauty
that invades, faithfully, all selves.

Brick-Hold

Only a frame and skin for the beating
of some lordly charge, it stands rhyme-sturdy
on a clay base — angular strips of grey
above square flesh, once signalled to provide
as a servant or spouse the necessary
ease and polish. Here is the check against
iron-shelled insects, creeping grasses
and oozing water. Behind a criss-cross
of insured fabric just those energies
are tended and tolerated: a fetid heap,
lice, roots and rain. Over the border,
of concrete maybe, a whitethorn blossoms
and the site is reversed, as your object
becomes frail controller over the years.

Supposes

Turn, counter-turn and stand: in slim glitter
we say we will move and are encased,
arranged by arm-rests and minding the gap
as, flicker-tense, a word lights up
reminding how with logs burning
the long-held scene is lived, out there
at the end of the road. It's a thought
that the soil would inhabit your face
and some quiet star might be breathed
away from this glandular throb.
Still the saxophone along the passage
is a voice of golden flesh, and if
identity slices with a rumble
one mask farther on is sense enough to wake.

Desire

Impossibly, the moment kicks that fool
into larking — was it a smile or some word
did it — and despite fear, a remembered stain
or maybe to show and rehearse it again,
the plunger slides into wholeness
crying here is home, a half lie
to tell all that's ever been, so something
is filled in the strange between.
Warm and sweet, for both in the mix,
a trice extends into forever,
only it is sure, equally, this bond
bears a price, as the once enveloped
knows no stop — until a stifling
drives one or other thick-skinned away.

Metabasis

Night's ribbon is cut and the stiff stretched line
is bent and lifted yards into forbidden space.
A bottle and a cannon exchange arcs
as history, chipped out, rolls
twenty frames a second, disproving
the cold imperative. Sentences point
with prominent breakage, showing horsepower
beneath mere bronze. In grainy squares
faces admit the day, once undernourished
and fearful, and hands clasp strange clothes.
From a shot despotism the open market sings
promising what you will, when a tense beyond
offers jockeyship and submergence
in anthems of blood or alluvial spirit.

Castlehaven

Round you the blocks are massed, body deep
and one voice of attachment eases
by laying three-pile on stone
so the name and property are shown.
Words stare unoccupied from every frame
and the figure outside beckons,
offering to fill a whole with part,
to irrigate and reopen the heart.
You turn with dishevelled hair,
moment-fed and carefree, eyes bluer
than Atlantic waves, and you step
across the scripted line
finding other chords to denote
the coincidence of mine and thine.

Sheet Bend

Strings of the small repeated day
we do not share — provisioning
and cleansing — as we knot ourselves
in a guise that holds and must give.
It's a lack and a gain to see you
fresh out of clocked allegiance
wearing fluid wraps of beige and black
to revamp the obvious and plain.
Without you, I'd say, any reading
is dead collected lines; with you
in context words get up and speak.
They press — uneasily — through the gap
and surge to find an expanse
that plucks farness into right here.

Touch-Paper

They cry we are lost in midnight tunnels
too far run into fortress rock.
They hiss it's a game in double language
wearing each face to blank mistrust.
But who can judge a line that twists
scorching with surprises, the slow caress
which builds to unburden, rosy
or ruinous in undying spillage.
If into eternity I am come
daring to break that perfect box,
and she with me says the breach is for joy,
let this sapping have bright issue
for the strongpoint where love and law engage
might torch a heaven in halls of adamant.

Possession

Even this belongs, a part that's foreign
to sense and ease, like the cat enclosed
with shining pitch that asks to be stroked
and left alone, staring through aeons
of granite. We tussle in a small chamber
furnished to make a world. Death-seeking
with a quiver and clench, we vie and ally
in concertinaed time, feeling by default
what we also are, as self-stages
spread from a hidden corridor
invoke Love's gilded capstone.
To steal into the present like this
makes a story where none exists,
one that's constantly beginning.

Old Redding

Some would make this threadbare, even
by aureate terms, but I must sing
from the heart-root, unclotted and clear,
naming how the plain builds to a height
which is special for all it holds.
We walk and lie in this last preserve
with its elbow paths and shaggy bushes,
watching from the pillared shade—
as masked horsemen—a sort of real day.
Grass stretches up from Copse Farm
and the Brick Field, while the sun catches
one spire on the hill. Windflowers here
are a drift of white and the yaffle pecks
his way north to Grim's Ditch and Levels Wood.

Field Figures

That there's only one is manifest
untruth: five in a hundred might offer
kindness or wit or beauty, a tongue
to divert with delicate strokes,
hair to entrain a wilder breath,
hands to know wherever what stirs.
But no other it seems will grip me so,
as war undergone in a tent on hard ground.
She opens and closes in a claret set
which implies some star-roofed redding,
though out of chance is built, slowly
the composition that's belonging.
Not all in the eye and pretty much made
she's a fitter mate than dreams relayed.

Middle Eight

Rising with you at the wrong end
of the day, flushed from sacrilegious tunes,
to hum down slippery surfaces
of no compare, I carry you back
to another life, breathless.
We are in a wild of hours
that is meant to not exist,
as if unmetered in strictest space.
Almost forgot to take my clothes off
today, lying right in you—
it is enough the words our fingers move
dispersing mist on a long highway
with just your perfume on my sweater
to always half remind me.

Tom Tiddler's Ground

How we got here, to a forgotten field
with its curtain of leaves and drop
to the fierce lips of the sea, was just
by a crossing of the older voice—
out from the hall with its turreted roof,
a hierarchy of grammar that sounded big
but needs an I-beam to join any thought.
(Betrayal is a blooded hand on the pillow
when you've made it through night's oriel.)
Now all April shines in her face
as the stalks hang limp after rain.
We're picking up lumps of gold: whoever
is caught, the game will go on, as present rights
rear insistent from the rut of measured speech.

Valentine

Say this is different from records of before
(buds to bareness letting crack fond words),
remember what holds as entered melody,
my fingers firm in your lightest down.
If the scales should tip and one half adopt
another wanted shape, an ingredient missed
in a leaden pull, may we take no loss
but wait till the whole revives, truly in refrain.
Don't block your heart and go off uncharmed
when I burn through all the keys of love,
don't bounce me as a first-born toy
when you tire of settled tablature.
Should I ever forget your latitude or leaning,
breathe into my lines a supple wax relief.

Numbers

One stands up with nothing to lose,
arrowed to grasp and go, keen-spined
for travel, wary but open
to joining. Rooted like steel
in the flat, carrying a thousand stories,
it yet is hollow and cracked
remembering how it was formed
in a burst of fine addition.

Two leans backward in shared habit,
bending its head with a swan's grace,
posits an overlay or exact fit
with different rates of expansion
when the heave beneath argues
sand and water one can't build on.

Dialogue

Cut this and go for the centre, anyhow
since the time is reduced to who eats what.

Your eye on the silver you'll just get slops.

Sit there frugally in thoughts of ought
and you'll never lay the course, know what is.

Better to be true in part than twist into undeeds.

The heart is the idea beyond — here done proud.

That quick shine suggests an eye disfigured,
a hollow strain in a monument.

I listen mesmerised but I will not stop.

If someone gave their palm full of hours
you wouldn't seize opportunity's forelock.

I'd see it rosefrail on a levelled line.

Which would hide the curve of the tongue in space.

The Call

Felled, you are, without a sign, my last prop
and first driver, taken somewhere sudden
I cannot believe, the line beneath all
the heard and glimpsed examples, a sleep
from which there's no removal, unless —
burnt and scattered — the spirit re-collects
what is undone and demands attention
as, stuck in dreams, you pass me the staff.

Survivor out of fire, I wear your clothes
(that other I patterned disorderly)
and reach for letters on the shelf you left
to keep a balance through watery days.
We stop to handle these things unsaid,
are pushed into tracing some new ascent.

Coordinates

To find words that render, unsmart with affection
what is brick-solid and shifting over clay:
this remains — to rake through the years
and imprint toughly those lineaments
which tell today where tomorrow is built.
I look up and there are four cold stars
splayed into a diamond — the Scales, his sign
of care and judgment, that guided my hand
on wood and metal. Whatever came out
I learnt the how in strokes, even to squeeze
the trigger like an orange. Shaping letters
I push with the left as he from battle
won back a world that fitted, precarious
with wealth and the chance to twice improve.

Dogdays

Your last scene you played quite away from the frame,
almost with no standers-by, one lonely duel
overheard as a gasp with night's postponeless foe.
I suppose he came an averted other,
irreversible, metallic, with a key
that skeletoned stuff held dear, echoing
where twice you'd been but for luck or grace.
You were readier than any of us,
went bravely into that maze of idleness
from a business packed and portioned.
To speak of this is some live extension
like a truer honour off-parade,
yet all the wires of memory
won't haul up ashes from a yard of turf.

After-Image

At first it was as if noun and verb
had changed places, and how could this not
disturb the relational cut, an implied
order of who talks to whom and when.
Five minus one—the king-pin—leaves parts
struggling for a new lay-out, stunned connectors
aligned to a print that is over-ridden.
Still in your easy chair, you are the teller
crystalling shrapnel and mud with a snatch
of Lili Marlene, a cup of 'Sergeant-Major's Brew'.
Poised appraiser of the vintage, you watch
as we, your scions, twine into drier fruit.
Here and not here, you will the quartet to work,
stress and strain creating a dialogue from home.

Impression

A film of dust is lifted: safe in boxes
the bright lead coats lie flat. Perhaps
none of us understood, running stiff
from the if only's of unit trust,
how a simple game sets the code for most
of what you do or don't. Breaking clear
depends upon the rule. To jump across
pavement slabs, to spill ink on one's jacket,
to stuff twigs down the waste-pipe —
these are the moves from self to self
which lead back to another belonging.
Not quite unsearchable, your kin-text
with its blocks, chinks and courses
will square out what slants to the final tip.

Matrix

Inchly out of silence a channel is moulded,
words not needed when all was in place.
A second learning between us comes strange
as implements are passed at breakfast
and cut news spreads thick with habit.
Now I grasp the colour of what I was
seeking, in a mirror of difference
time after time: she would spark fantastic
stepping out for the dance, she would breathe
concern through the last reel, so my model
was weight if lightly held. I went warring
on a frozen pitch, bathed in a friendlier pool,
but each performance against the grain
was an echo of this earlier script.

Utility

Not to have trodden the wanted path
out to the car and the meeting
of associate steel, not to have
worn creases and stripes which
set one apart but among, not to have
drunk the terms and spawned angel
terrors, not to have made the here
and now emit . . . tulips in cement?
But to have slipped past the rockery
and pergola, looking for another
language, words sunk in the stream
to refloat and reposition:
Is wealth pushed into a larger moment
got by some sullen wreck of easiness.

Transport and Misnaming

What is the river that edges up
on this inner brick? A stream in the wood
long blocked and flattened. A word chosen
from there to tell what's happening here.
The scene you build is sealed but it slips
somewhere else. Shades alter like salt
on the wall, however exactly red.
My grid is a hold-all that glistens
with particular faces: the lips and eyes
he followed from a smelt blouse, her search
for hands which speak and listen, dual blood
which converts to another the same.
If it's a kind of wrong, it gets to be true
as the stars on the day you decide.

Aspic

Snaking relentless out of rain and snow,
other seasons and stories, it thrusts
between scorching walls and spills wider
giving the strip that sustains — a country
of green and red richly black, a coming
and going moved by a muddy star to prompt
the curved lip of the lily that avenues
back to its maker's sigh, its user's song
as proof of rest after toil, long-slow
like points joined on the sky's ceiling
for a bark's journey through reeds
and stone triangles, its sail outstretched
to soar, a hawk's wings angling
berry-blue in the desert's double fringe.

Privily

You see, or think you see, through the lens
every single hair, indigo vein and salt pore,
all the crags and valleys of a blown life
windowed for scanning in tabloid layers.
Here is your evidence, names and so on
that promise a route to the underside self:
what was readily done by a rhododendron
out on the weald one night in June.
It could be the story explains the picture,
some retranslation into first feeling.
But behind the wordface is another
made up, a tone which trades with the stuff
it creates, subjecting flesh by a sleight
which hides how one leads back to many.

Uncollected

1992–1994

Minor Concerns

Who are the people who are sneering, saying it's a little idea . . . It is surely sensible that standards should be publicly set and measured, that managers and providers should be challenged to do better and, above all, that the users of services should be able to compare their end-results.

John Major

I is an other
apostrophe for possession
in iron:
getting it better
a little curve
clocking the pupil
back to before.

Any body can buy
next to the next
significant player
the optimum means
to forget

increase by losing
an extension of franchise
when the word
belies arrangement.

Your mother,
a pretty good imposter,
said she knew
each item's cost
and would keep it there

despite the maker's wage
or the colour of
what's downstream.

Red, white and blue
the habit of choice

is a second or third
generation truth:

the tried and trusted
is not history
but nature

so the looked-for spread
brooks no argument.

(Not the question but the terms
are territory removed
from the map of where
one would want to go.)

Lords is ever the defining crease
with which country you cheer
the final test of native:
sustain with those admired
a bronzed idyll

but climbers in the garden
point a different sense
of normal — tugging to retrieve
Victorian with pliers.

Dream of the track
and a chugging guarantee
of local, while fixers
put in believable props.

Best on the table is
the mallard, shot
below the high-water mark
or whatever available
imitation
can be often thought.

Don't let your interlocutor
speak between lines

it's a remit to rip
the dawn.

Not really a heel
the citizen treads
that line in the corridor
chartered for an easier deal.

All of most move
to a sliding schedule
which powers the user
by reduced service.

Hearing about the odd win
no assessment reveals
whose future
is cash positive.

A lot's been given away
a lot's been taken —
one grammar is not up
to knowing.

Yule flushed
in the bare ward
where lines of time
reach warmly
through a little clench
and glazed stare

He is the puckered cry
of possibility
against the metal beds
and stiff cloth

Wealthy with other stock
wizened and smooth
he is the father
brought back to light
dull hearts
in a radio join
over London
fir and slate

for Peter Guy Astbury, born 25.12.93

Byrd Consort

for Caroline Trevor

Sing your part at the feast
    over twelve days
in the Great Hall
    a crowd pressed
by belief to wonder & hide

Mind makes a kingdom
    in twelve-foot hole
fury stepped aside
    out of orient skies
a blazing star will shine

By composition (contract)
    five viols take up
from chest to air
    bite clear on tune
arm to leg, gut-rich trance

Pour as rain off lead spout
    all wistful-grave
above rose brick
    to wind Moorish
in deep a rifled undersong

Argue to rest, and rejoice
    the leaves be green
as a lady's secret
    and nut browning
beyond in walled garden

De Luce (reprise)

Was by the pond is inside the silt. Fathomly
fingering the stalk. Swords bound
upward at ease. A cloak spread
for boats, buoyant and fleshy.
Lean tiptoeing on the slats
of what tiny bridge We (They) were
at a distance laughing. Birds.
No others to ask. Her diadem of him
a resolution of one vowel into two —
that blue corduroy dress loosing
townlessly as skin goes white.
Sing lie-la-lie, the bulb
is a sun-spoke to know, she says
not taking the petals apart.

from **Roxy**

1985–1996

1

Wrought in moonshine nights
dance the measures
trick of learning
the violet-bed
the banquet of sense
dew on the rose
clings about.

Wear it, she said, this viscose —
we extend ourselves into the actual,
the object of the quest has changed,
not its meaning.

You think this is counterfeit
but we go vizarded with intent
as close corners of the heart.

Layer upon layer
the longing dazzles.

Does the body end with the skin
portraits of the state we're in?

Come make yourself different:
thoughts woven with fancy's shadows
to bear a part in a swelling scene.

Alexanderplatz, under the railway —
rich silk, soft linen and cool cotton —
he wanted her there

a musk and amber base
jazzing block by block
its bindings
as stripes and bars rewrite the figure.

It is the rhetoric of history,
Clio's oils and gems

Pushing object into subject,
it seems after centuries
she inhabits her house.

She dresses to please
herself, down décolleté
with burnished-leaf earrings
and a diamanté choker,
stretched lips and blown hair.

He breathes
uneasy to rule
establishing shots:
Live in Anytown
Among the Darkers
Rampant Syncopatio
Old Wax and New Waves.

Show me what rouge you wear
and I will tell you
who you are.

A country domed with star-galleries —
her banks, hedges and highways
embroidered with eyes.

Drinkable gold
includes Destination Venus
with beat madness selector,
steel tips echoing
as the street enters the house
and gang fashion is high fashion.

Brought the apache into the Ritz,
hinted a fusion of pilferings:
slattern powder and B-movie anecdotes
shimmying from the inside
surrendering sleeze charm,
stack heels and sequins,
each line a punch.

There should have been more jungle
not so much girl.
I wanted the steamy feel of the jungle,
a certain ratio
bereft of name, home, history.

When you have taken the skin off the earth
how she will breathe.

With borrowed pulse
stamped on the retina
the streets belong to everybody:
glam-trash, asset-strippers,
patchwork anything

the silk plumage
translated into commodities
and frozen.

Pecuniary canons:
who gasps over a bench
in the sweating den.

Puritan ghosts to the chameleon—
smoke in history
from the Triangle Shirtwaist fire.

All tied up with Thou Shalt Not
till buckling the burden catches:
a bit of unfairness, lady,
to keep people on their toes.

Aurora Backseat
moves from the didactic to the hallucinatory,
glazes the shifty identity
as desire displaced
a rigid abstract shell.

You cannot cloak this when you spring
out of a dull tinted brokery
aiming to seem a winner:
the man who drives the crowd,
meat in his eye
a manifesto,
knows his own imperatives.

5

The set was too real
so they brought in a crack-painter
and a tree-painter
(the Japanese do it all the time).

We shot it through a silk stocking
because we wanted it to look dry
and we hoped to knock down
that green look.

The music was in romance time,
I don't think we after-eighted it.

9

What Cleopatra did, when the season urged it,
to bring the seas into her throat.
What is obtained with the greatest hazard.
What lies deeper than sunbeams.
What spreads with a kind of gaping.
What is filled with prolific dew.
What is white, smooth and round.
What dangles from fingers and ears.
What rattles with Indian waves.
What, liquefied, lost Antony his wager.

12

From babbling days we crawl
on flat floors through vertical doors
in a familiar terror that excites
as now the struts hum a kind of tension
with a glass slab of who's in charge
stilted over your heritage encounter,
one trap of hell 'undamaged' by concrete piling.
There is a canopy of signs on Bankside —
a shadow thrown up by pneumatic pounds
charged at three removes from the absent user.
One says it's poetry, another the show
as they wrangle whose name should go first.
It slowly comes to be repeating,
a laid-on feast, a ribbon of blood
as the hands climb up to midnight.
Breath please! Can we do this to ourselves,
backed by the ghost of morality,
fronted with half the nerve to defy it?

Wanting control, we pin all hope
on a special decorum, the long view,
like coronation notes in a deletion society,
or we go with fast-track, bolt-together dreams
in pink and khaki, high on enterprise.
There is no chucking the language —
it's a dialogue with the father,
with bears displaced in the raked yard
and baiting alive again.

It seems just a face with nothing inside
when you recall the lightness and poise
that came with exact calculation,
when streets were in the air
and all spoke from a right-angled geometry.
But our emergence from concrete and steel
is more than a stutter-step, a dash
surrounded by a contradiction.

Say it's the same with different 'ands an' eyes,
a pressing on with more colour, there is an after
which we won't dispute, run together in printing,
so the subject sits apart from the pointed new
with a flicker of humour and a choice of stops.
If out of bombing a corporate vision of white
gave us stained panels, and if the architect
has always said 'I', this is rightly associational
(a resplendent 'one of us' with a touch
of people's detailing). Marketing meets aesthetics
isn't the whole story, for we had to break out
with warmer materials — a mixture of wood and brick,
grained like skin and easy-jointed, giving off
a recognized scent and glow. The ache is
how to dress, with values based on congestion
and a style cumulatively rigid. You need surprise
yet it's got to be readable — rooms and corridors
at least hinting their use, roofs and walls
suggesting an interior destiny.

The turrets are ears, the windows eyes
and the furnace a stomach — a dream which portends
fire, perhaps. Give over, voice — the reading
is problematic. I wanted a plan that lets in
kitchen smoke, guest gossip and baby talk,
an evolution in gear with wattle and daub,
and I wanted the space to work out
furious pictures. Assailed by new money
and lager cries, I thought there was shelter
beneath the stilts. But that friendliness
was loaded from the start, as offices hung over
what might have been home. To make sense
there has to be another way of telling it,
the pieces arranged in a curious pattern
moving arguably beyond the sellable
so the seer isn't message-fodder.

Imagining carbuncles on a trusty countenance,
with years tracked on the brow,

our guardian reverts to a safer handsomeness,
in a throwback gesture which disguises
where blood has been spilled
(and sperm and wine). The tire-man rules,
importing shapes designed in different light,
different weather. By this we evade
the monstrous climax and take on
a sepia integrity. The life in the words
lies slack, as the spandrel is not up
to carrying the figure. An apparent quiet
is recorded: the busking iron beneath
and the pigeon-filled sky have not been heard.

I kicked the bottles and tins,
fragments on a barren walkway,
and I too needed to run. I saw
sweet-wrappers as seed-pods, emptied
of their last blessing. The smile retreats
as muggers and pushers swivel into
an almost sanctioned market-drive.
(Promises on the home front may fool
those at the rally and some who pay less
for alarm-strewn villas.)
Leaving the bridge, I was not above it all:
could see how the syntax was meant to work,
with Lego bits urged into play —
a neat solution to an old nightmare.
But in two decades the lift was a sewer
and rage was pinioned by despair.

And now they're dynamiting one block in ten
or tarting them up with a fountain,
a pitched roof and video security.
When the message is special the demand alters:
what was spurned is prized. You shift a word
and the filing cabinet is lightened.
(It was not meant for children, anyway.)
There'll be no shortage of takers
as the self is inflated to fit the grid,

for we breathe and heave appointedly
by a corresponding mathematic.
Let's not forget—there are ten million
at the bottom of the heap
holding a version of soap.
But behind the gut-felt complaint
is a voice disowned, receptive to climbing
in pure steel.

Freed from load-bearing, the wall
has a thousand windows—sections of space
bounded by four lines. Compare the Disney smile
of clamped-on symbols: exaggerated eyebrows
above goon-specs and a candy-filled mouth.
It's a joke of mirrors, pillaging
from the disregarded. To do it with grace
or to please the liver in a wittier lapse
you'd have palms leading to a brace of turrets.
Most, if not all, are implicated
as the quick buck dances with newness
and two storeys are added each fortnight.

In the swell of a double code the assumption
can slip: the too-pondered phrase
is limiting—a mural of the five senses
dreamt in the Liberty of the Clink.
You recoil from belief as the giants float by,
girded from rust with a coat of gold.
Fame is here to disperse rumours
and only love may be spoken of
when the organ booms across an aftershow
of clapping. Pepper's ghost still has a grip:
that haunting tune is a reminder of torn halves,
a signal gone ahead of use, under-believed in
and shortly applied, or a mass-digested moment
at ninety-nine pence, a slice of heart
extended in defiance and tied with tape.
Number One is a promise nicked by the enemy,
and it's the place you want to stop.

14

I dreamt of the city of books,
its ten great halls
composed in white, with veins alive
through altered skin,
of numbered and titled passages
where mice and worms made barely a meal,
of ingathered leaves
from which all ages spoke,
as Cleopatra feasted Caesar,
of an involuntary flame
that ripped through the wharfs,
and the meaner final dispatch:
Omar's decree that either way —
against the prophet or not —
such works were redundant,
so that six months' fuel was provided
for the public baths.

26

To begin again with screeches and feedback,
we all have clock numbers and the spur of poverty.

They said it was streamlining
and they closed twenty mills.

Starved of capital,
chafed by import penetration,
offered no breathing space,
the industry slides into outward processing —
a foreign fabric cut by laser
and sent back to be sewn and finished.

Only a vertically integrated multinational
is geared up to survive,
with paint, packaging and plastics
as well as the wood pulp to make its fibres.

Another he, another she
are stretched by market oscillation,
forces unfettered,
their flesh darts an extension
of telephone-figure salaries.

Money tightens the muscles
as each room is personalized.
By a promissory note they create
a lived relation out of nothing,
its resemblance unchallenged,
not in this dimension.

With more information and less knowledge,
they have original features in a prime location:
a glazed storm porch, a lawn area
plus apple, pear and cherry trees;
an en suite avocado bathroom
and twin reception rooms,

with recessed spotlights,
coordinated colouring
throughout.

Or they have a starter home
with warm air heating,
a fenced off patio area
and a fully tarmacked forecourt.

Isn't it about time you changed your car?
Why, are the ashtrays full?

Ours has soft-touch buttons.
Seduce them with the name —
you've got to be in love with your product.

The entryphone rings in a fitted bedroom.
The market works if left to do so,
say the buzzards, whose best friends
are inaccessible. With added leverage
an illusory hands-off is sustained
to inflate values, as half way to Paris
the butter mountain freezes
into perpetual craving (gold one cannot eat).
It's a taste engrafted into the system:
when he has all he is not full.

On the finance page the gates are adorned,
the description is interlaced so an approach
is barely possible. Wrapped and strapped,
the information brokers vent their news
but don't tell how each man an investor
sorts with birthright or by what niggardise
and intermeddling the trim show is upheld.
Those who join hands around the base
can be sugared out of the musical.

Authority is the byword of freedom
and the green is made a commodity

as if it wasn't enough to have a house
behind every tree.

Lust, Pride and Envy strut through the city,
their faces thick with greasepaint—
a part taken for a whole—as actors applaud
the impression which only actors produce,
acting upon some act that is bent into a truth.

It could be yesterday, the pack that hid
their selves in women's dress
to beat a watchword senseless,
those that parade and do not parade
the overburdened member.

George's mound is fought for
by freeholders gnawed into resolution,
and there, in coffee-table glass, are enclosed
a dozen shots of wilderness Britain.

You forget about compassion, as if that decade
had never unravelled, let alone the one before.
You ematiate to rebuild the household stuff,
two nations sharp-set on a single river.

28

To pay the rent and electricity
she decided to go raw for a while.
Not to be misjudged, the punters bought champagne
and talked mostly of washing-machines.
With the other girls she was merrier than hell.

She had tiny bows on the back of her shoes
which suggested the word undone.

Dipping to another level,
it's all got a bit of fladge in it:
by the gaslight she was angelic,
a translation of adolescent fears.
The number was 'Jolene',
an extremely bizarre a cappella
sung in German throughout
with one spectator.

Her nipples were covered with pearls
and a winding sheet.
She held him off to make him hungry,
wearing function and symbol—
a limited edition.

In the club they said secretly
it doesn't seem worth the bother
of putting them on.

29

I am the voice in the shuttle
telling out of cut parts and zigzag joins
a story you'll try to deny:
gold got in a dark cave,
sweat-work to ravish your eyes.

With Care, the critic and Eagle
watching every stitch,
with a loop of heartaches singing
'please, don't take my man'
and 'brokedown angel blues',
I do my job to the best
twisting crimson into white
as a riddle someone might see.

There's hardly a stop for fumbles
with time chalked on the wall.
Arms and fingers, numbly nimble,
pull and press in a dogged throb
strange to the millionth repeat.
You and your monster, lashed to the bench,
tilt in a kind of miracle act,
keeping the bundles moving,
more alive with each tuck and slit
for the hanger to carry it off—
a standing lie or prodigious riot,
whatever you're willing to think.

It's clammy as hell down there
with a stale vent to swish up air.
Neon streaks dustily across pale green
intended to soothe and revive
but the whir and judder bore through
to your bones and brain
and your eyes get locked in a bloodshot stare
till the bell goes for tea.

Sewing your self into the stuff,
you dream you'll wear it to the ball:
a white net skirt with a wide waist-band
to float you through to morning.
But with thorns and thistles as an instrument
you won't be rid of the curse.
The shine you get is just a machine
and the fun of a crazy tune.
Off-the-peg laughter is what you'll buy
to be out on the town tonight.

I could be nothing, an insect
whose slender limbs work up a curious web,
a shelter or trap for the wearer
who tries to possess such art.
Starlike, my knot of tongues
is a pearly shroud avowing what is done
or to do, almost notelessly.
Wracked at the window of another's hold,
dropped so deep from chummery,
we'll bob or crawl to the ledge again
looking to span the stone-space
which kept our words apart.

31

As you came from that other land
didn't you see her by the way?
A voice like the nourishing air,
a face to enlume night and day —
she who touched me, the child within
standing in a moment of fear.

Let me have that strain again,
kindred chimes in a gash of energy,
a carer who knows where to place each finger,
somewhere between need and want.

She is in a cornfield with the lightest breeze,
or by a mossy tree that leans over a stream.
She fills my silence with no overspill,
cooking ideas and sewing a word-chain.
She does a turn in time, opening
a counterpart, and infolds odorously
to grasp lineaments of joy.

Mutual maker, trusty and fresh,
she goes her own road extended,
as warbling notes emerge from dense cover
and tender stalks stretch unnumbered
into sun-streaked mist.

Can you do no better than recite
what is heaped from old endeavour?
I would be there if language
had not split me, if salesmen
had not drawn me, self-clutching
on a pedestal imparadised, a mile
from the floor of workaday seams.
It, they, set my breasts too high
and I bully you, a corner of worship
in my heart, unable to trust the lyric voice
as other than headed notepaper,

clangily portentous like the brass flock
on Assurance Hill. How I yearn,
in amnesia almost, for the landed age
which accompanies the label,
for strong-lined verses
that are more than tropes, less than gush.
You look for the one right word
in imperishable garb, when handy-dandy
your cook and sew, made proper in proper
can't turn the roles around
or negotiate appearances.

I thought that I was an entity
present placed as sound, that you
were the one apart, dressed to meet
assumption, a recognized voice
in the plot that carries us on,
but you is another I, holding so
to keep whole as all assaults
the ear. You could say you know
they were joined at the mouth
with sushi-tongues, I mean
the rule is suggestive, she and he
are breaking the code in silent gesture,
an instant free converted from goods to flesh
and back, for there is always a third
hurled beyond exact verity, like movie gods
in a stretched limousine. I gave myself
as total return, seeing her in her
and this in this, an intimate I shrugged off
to envelope, aching to lose and find
in an hour-glass crossover
that is now fashion's forsaking,
home that is not home.

You talk of endings where none
have arrived, a penny-blood version
of the touching display. If I'm a ghost-child
in returning fits, the elusive wrap

on your stretched stave, if I'm a seabird
with a slate-blue skirt, inked
into an interim reading, I am as much
rubbed reality, what starts
at the petal's edge: five-foot-five,
eight-and-a-half stone, 34-25-36,
with a 'C' cup and a size five shoe,
hazel eyes and straight hair,
one mole at the side of my neck.
First I am — bones, organs, muscles and skin,
much like you and different, under glamour
and the nibbling of chocolate, as I juggle worlds.
There is a place, a part, I want and do not want
you to go, somewhere beyond my heart,
an oval or a circle which could be
the wreath of flowers and greens
tied round the top of my crib,
a little out of focus, never blank.

I drove you blind into the night
wanting to crash and wanting to come through,
with rain beating in harmonica dreams,
quavery and long-sustained, in an urge
to find my own pitch. I was the clown,
I was the hero, pushing my bulk
in a narrow theatre, silly and brave
in one manageable frame with bubbles of thought
leaking through devilment. I won you
and treasured you, building from and against
a remembered softness, and maybe I was tamed
in my ivy jacket and wood grain trousers.
Was it a one-sided idea of home,
some fussily attentive arrangement
with he and she mugs, spin-dry kisses
and a tick and a cross of rehearsed lines?
I carried the spiders out and bolted the door,
thinking you wanted me well-behaved,
then you went for the heel that crunches glass,
a gaoler in a black-and-silver uniform.

It was — your words — a magnificent slip,
falling ice-red into stuff not done.

Once I trembled and took you in, thrilled
at your no-curves, punchy solid and hot
like ash bending into farthest naught.
Your story act was the best, laughing me
into riffs of desire, so it did not stop
with your ending but went on
by invisible eddies, a slang
that you almost can't speak —
you might have to blank me here —
a sweet sting of anything, tight and slow,
my legs wrapped around your neck,
a slimy reptile in the race memory,
a visiting god in foliage.
You drew the poison out of me,
bore the brunt of my late alarm,
wrestled equally in wordstock,
understood in one slip of a smile.
You let me brood — apart — and yet were there
to talk and talk, down to the matt black
in an over-sea of dulnesses, giving no easy
it'll-be-alright but sparking me on
to walk with pronoun courage.

Yours was a function, mine had to be learned,
bought and re-won, in sectors of some old adventure,
as regents clapped or jeered, slung forward
by a pontoon crossing, with one ace in reserve,
to join texts in echo of the merger,
recklessly investing a hard-to-say brilliance
in that small cleft of country, where out of breath
I was a full-grown me, ready to lead and serve.
I got your wire, zingy in seven seconds
as you toyed with your glass then dipped
the throatline of your shoe. I wasn't just after
the label, god, your eyes were a smile which bespoke
legends of come-away put in the here and now,
a thinking beyond thought, where the big load

is shifted, with wit in each finger touch
and mettle in the slightest whisper. You held
my glance, not desperate or needy, and took
a whole history on trust, giving at your pulse points
something else, eagerness with wings, the scent
a man would climb for. Your lips, you said,
were mulberry, and in my sky-days I was off on that
(as always), though part of the taste is gone.

Dressed in horticolours, what did you want
me to advertize, a lioness with a word-habit
pouting in sub-classic lines, cute and coy
by your strong silence, primed to give
so much and so little, answering Mayday calls
when you were not fighting to land.
I won't deny I needed you to choose, sunk
in the labyrinth of my selves, wondering how
to present each scene. And it was more – far more –
than an honorary place in a short adventure.
Others have not done it, in temper and texture,
stiff behind laws in a romper-room. Oh there'll be
a fine cut of trouser, a glimpse of short hairs
rising at the back of a neck, the right spice even,
but it will be down to me to ease things along,
chirping bla-bla-bla to the original Mr Shutmouth.
With that snugness of weight – cool hard planes –
I'll spin as a daughter, disremembering how
I was the prettiest woman there and all you did
was stare beyond our table, thinking some one –
my sister – would twist the flame higher. Well,
it was unrepeatable and, I guess, worth the going-on.

Let the images play: we know the story and still
forget what happens, as it hangs on the if
of hoops and streams, looping from laughter
into sadness. I numbered every frame, listening,
and you moved away; I let the strip burn, deaf,
and you moved away. You said the one who rings
is the least desired and you cried out for news
(my so-called better nature). I was a hint

of hoochie-coochie for your sliding mercury,
a chip apart from the boardroom brain. Damn it,
you always said right when you meant left
and it was funny, like go away a little closer,
when I hurled a pint of Guinness in your face,
reddening your eyes and staining the wall,
while you knocked my glasses into space
so neither of us could trace the cause. Oh, how
I relished your cunning—the game in your iris
or ear-lobe—and mostly you said there's a kid
beneath the wolf, in realization of actual size.
Barricaded, we escape, roving, we home in,
as he and she, me and thee, shift places
in the river and tower of grammar.

If I've only one life, let me live
as a blonde, with chance wisping out
as unattributable voices,
concealing to reveal, revealing to conceal,
yet not coldly observed
like all the shop windows to world's end.

Let me be safely frightened
with lions and tigers licking my breasts —
one man enough to fire vision
and soft enough to inspire service,
defined neither as a cluster of consonants
nor as a flush of Italian vowels,
for the heart has many fashions.

I remember the glassy hill he climbed
for me, and the mirror that seemed
to shatter, a secession that co-opted
our language, when he put too much
hind self in this, so I drifted
to a dead-pale border with no increment
of experience, the one I am untellable.
And he sent out a code of refined despair
as I permed the wires of revision.

32

The world lies open, a double slab.
It's still to be done, or already done,
a mildewed hoard with a cracked hinge
still holding. It's a fortress
or mortuary temple
that yet has marks which stalk
the landscape.
There's a deep blue entry
to horizontal rows,
a script which contains
only itself and more.
You could come to the same
along simple paths
perhaps, with punctuation
starting to bud.

34

Heretical figures put our concepts on trial.
Have we eaten the heart, to have no other taste?
I had a dream till a movement killed it,
I had a movement till a dream killed it.
I was an actor warming frozen words.
I was a word warming a frozen actor.

A revolution of 180 degrees
is the sentence coming into being.
Who, then, is the cell animator?

Production is the watchword now
structured for the average reader,
whatever that means. With workers redundant,
golden apples are comfortably outlandish
if they're printed right into the gutter.

To speak with sense
you hold your nose or your purse.

The soul's palace is erected wit
without any sparkle of light.
Her diverting parts are a piece
of mere manage, an idea twirled
into a costly thatch.

Take off this value-language
for under that you may see beauty.

Gold and silver. You speak as if
they were an illusion and the orchard not.

I'd rather set myself in your green-house
than in the cold gallery of fashion.

It was settled once with bottles and chairs,
by a landrover driven up a poet's boot.

That was before helicopter blades
lifted the pages of corporate ink.

Flying with the last drop, there's no further
to go on. It's a heart map, a fool's head world.

Oil beneath tracing sings a hymn momently
coloured to cry what's new.

Feathers are a burden, unfinished as fable
and tranced into a glaze.

You can hide with floating letters.

The voiced valise is no picture
but sometimes a tool to point the pretence
it's convenient enough to follow.

We walk dumpily away from the drivel
while others cover, endow, commit.

In the end they're all the same —
just different uniforms.

Style is what you can't deny
about yourself.

36

From cotton fields to the catwalk
you look for the master trope
in a lexicon of fopperies.
Nobody knows what's nice or not—
it's whatever compels belonging.
Fabric gives birth to what you want.
Nitrate crumbles to dust.
The more of the moment you are
the more of the past you become.
All grammars leak: the end of the silk road
is an animal print shirt
reassuringly dear.
Leaves eaten by a worm
are the memory of a world
without memory.

40

Who should she by goodgrip assayal
disclose? A derivation. Leaden, orificial
as bark freed from the tree.

Nobody's something makes alike
our rendition. 'Ragged but right.'

Pointedly. An accident. Carries
the song. Down. A ways.

Giggling, she takes the pin
and they go through-stitch.

Tight but not too tight
she ramps a mythy habit.

Torqued so, by what
does she ad-dress?

A web to be worn or swept away.
A winged angel with a terrorist in front.
A vial that spills into unwished sense.
A river cutting black through a white desert.
A box of leaves that'll gape from one side,
flutter and buzz. A piece of vacant lumber.

Mockable, into the wood I vouch
my terms, better to say they're so.

46

Are these words to act, printed in the mind
as a building? Forecourt, hall, arch,
living room, dining room, stairs,
bedrooms, bathroom. Demand from a statue
what is hitched to the stars,
rouse the demon from black diamond doors.
When we're afraid we forget. Instead
let the stiffs unroll, what you did
or might have done, a zigzag
made by shafts of light.
Read it at a glance, a single glyph
that calls down worlds.
Pull hell or heaven from a drawer.
Listen to a sounding vase.

A room is defined by the properties.
These might be a table with books, a chair.
He talks to himself through the pages.
An angel points, his body cropped,
forbidding, another wills him on.

Sleeves stripped up like a juggler,
he argues the case, vulgarly
to scowls and mumbles, steps into fire
for a kiss, or wisdom.

When you gravel the scoffing
is there ever a blue skies option?

Uncover, measure the chalk
of robbed out walls, bare bones
of the geometry, two inches high.
It's a polygon that can pass itself off
as a circle, a flower bounded by
a ditch and sewer.

Money behind money scoops in mud
for a renegotiated view, lines where
'they' won't tread:

Something's in the bud, moves
invisible. A candle-man
under flying cranes.

Don't say the joke isn't part of the scheme.
Mean and grovelling a meal vanishes —
chickens and pudding with 'This is mine'.
Paid for a slice, he hacks his way
to the source. Long for, burn, re-mark
all the perfumed verge, a distant cast
for an always return.

A phrase out of the charred leaves
says make the moon your plot.
Unlogged, intenser, an eye runs
on the ridges, stretches across
lead-in-white, brimming her quiet
thin-thickness, a platform
for invention. To click an icon
and go over, to cut a door
beyond the flaming limits.

Dread the spotlight in a black box
but it sleeks the scene
to a fine divide.

Falling apart in paraphrase
what's seen and allowed
is the tacit middle, a freelance voice
without all the answers.

He awes the I
longer lived in storm-clouds:
her likeness is everyone and no one,
snatches of another

entirely yours
turbulent in stand oil.

She looses for
effects as affected, pressed
red accents to his black
frame — a wound like wine
on crusted shelves.

Westering, in the rummage
each one fainter, she smiles
a range of selves, proffers
the isolate clasp or scarf
that set off blood-rushes.

Slender fingers, the glaze
of more, and the nerve
to walk on through.

Curious this way or that
after the deed an hour is a year
over and over, a single sole
on the stair of love,
a frenzied climb on a slow map.

Suppose she's come back to cloud.
Beasted, he holds an empty robe.

Petals of a name that pleases.
Soprano atoms — the score
to raise a city.

Levelled in the subplot
there are still wings rising
in alabaster — if you can stick
the smoke. Words played in the head
from pillars and a painted backdrop
live as dust of a round and square intention.

Numbers set the fashion
with hell's teeth and a tapering tongue
at four o'clock. Beer and bread
is the stuff, as a poet pleads
for indian silk. It's a rite
put on by a land-pirate, voices lost
in the mix and reverbing. A crack in the fabric
startles, ground to sky, as you'd think
wordishly it wouldn't, but the fit
copied by ear or dropped
with clay pipes and orange pips
clues any spirit to attend.

Watching a lyric face one class sweats
into the armpits of another.

47

Out of the waste you can spin
a garment of memory, coarser
than an episode in chiffon. It'll reach
between moods, pliant with a grammar
that's never complete. Now enfolds
then—a blip of smalltalk rendering
whole arabias of enchantment, with golden air
in drooping grey. Carry the flamingo
in spear-grass and tongues of acacia,
by a crooked vein over scorched plains.
Venture a life, awake to the gathered yarn,
out-fitting numbers. You go as the spiral
of storks above. Slaggy waves, chance pools,
forests of reeds and ferns, balsam-scented
silence, a crescent of scaly crags
snowcapped. The find is in the dream
by side-steps, fever and a little wild honey:
hail melting at noon. You have it as a child
in the book, if it's not burnt. Mist
over purple pinnacles. Set so
one word brings on another
like dancers hand in hand.

52

Hungry bower of drolleries —
bonework the lie to all —
street-sharp, invention
and wanting more.

Counterfeit, composed, affected,
outside the Big Agenda.
A pair of shoes, a chart song.
An expression not an opinion.
Designer myriads pranked up
speaking in the carriage of their bodies
(dumb shows and prognostics).
Not about necessity but choice:
colours of heavens, stars, planets.
Potent enticers
want to step out.

We are tiffanies, ruff-bands,
coronets, amulets, knots and swimming figures,
juggling strength of metals, stones, odours —
the flash puissant, the lingering cinnamon bark.

Go for sweet surfaces of added value,
take it to the limit
and quit before it peaks.

from Danse Macabre

1996

Summoned from work, day on night, who's the dancer
conning? A touch on the arm or shoulder: 'We were once
what you are. What we are you shall be.' Great with oversight
this swaggerer keeps no calendar. A face out of the funnies
in triplicate grins at a life extended like Zisca's drum.
Got to meet him in that day, return his smile. A bug-word,
a letter edged in black. We dared this with claused colours
painting the voice. One hour makes all alike.

Oil and labour spent, voyaging into data. What promises
rub out the figure in stone and glass. Paradise too uncertain
to be marked. Words thump in the ear to get beyond
loss or accident. Scanning to order the lay of the case,
a font of knowledge strikes from one mind to another,
a green lion grasping the means. Who would follow
down this tunnel or linger ahead? The frisket bites,
the carriage runs in to the second mark.
. . . . .

Love is being locked up. With a wedge, a quoin. Held space
of the page. Against the drift. A gold-tooled binding. Hell-pledge.
Receiving an impression with force she lies in the coffin
that will be him. Rhymed to death as halves of a perfect heart.
Love is being loosed. With a stick to reap. Kiss-tight
in the galley, to be ink-moist and through into the hanging,
Heaven-fold and dispersal. Our wits stretched out,
we are mischief for the taking, wisdom prized in play.
. . . . .

That joker got lucky, beyond the rafters of his body, dust
worn pages. A few steps here is a welcome break. Room for a dose
of enchantment. They clip with tuned tongues, tilt the engine
of the world, frisk against *decora* and the grave sentence
whirlingly by tinted panes. But talk to him tomorrow
and the massive frame, the wooden screw and straight bar
are broken monuments. Those eyes, those hairs, those hands
are an echo coarsed in the courser's record.

The fourth in the background has no double, he's died
enough times already or he's the innocent here, pounding
his bauble for Minerva. He's the scape that may not alter the sense.
Two deaths lean in tune with the uniforms, left-handed to take
this batch out of circulation. The other, whose sprigs of hair
and fleshier mask could signal the absent female, bonds equally
with the leaning pressman. Death's finger points each function out
either side of the post. Hemispheres to be divided in time.

Uncollected

1995–1997

Capricho Oscuro

Black cloak dream of blood red cloud
morisco veins in glass
reach to conquer
and convert
torn back
as joke of a book forbidden

blissed landing
from Algiers dungeon
serviendo la causa
to white carpet
under green crest

fiesta, ointment to galls
then a fever steeple

pipes
drums
a chirping echo
to the plat of crackers
and pound
of Micalet bell

chant
before
jewelled
cup

might *pícaros*
in a clean square
translate
this rough
journey

Still Saraband

i.m. Jan Lubelski,
Costa Blanca, 1.9.95

I

She on the shore, dipped already,
reads, in aura removed
from the churning sound-house
as her man and their sculptor friend
go again to test and relish
that jade liquid frontier. A brood
of forgiven argument lingers,
four-bar phrases throb as the wind
sighs into sand, gravely arching
to exact requital. Another loop
forms on water and cries
two solo in strained performance
fear with welter and chafe
she cannot heed such muster.

II

Gravelly billows drive
blue-green tiers, majestic
in wake of storm, a drift
local with heave of stranger gods
to lure in late fierce sun
a keen floater or two
kicking weed under froth
plucked weightless away.

What it keeps on saying
the flood we can't decipher,
carved restless, ridge to trough
trough to ridge, in limbo,
is — *land-locked and tideless*
the mythic laugh will strike.

East of Absolute

for G.E., dark
in the filmic brief

Just any taste it is
not, I swear
when you rib my nights
recorded before
as if this were less,
some desperate habit.

No, it's the juice
of a burst pomegranate
and if I more haggardly
rise against the myth
that seems, give me
the swell, the allowance
to give, not most by words
but somethingly so—by default.

Exile Dawn

Talk me to sleep
with tales
on your purple leather sofa
in Belsize Park.

The judge won't tell
who the daughter is
and under the rose
your cat I swear smiles.

It's a long way back
to Clare and Kerry
but blink and the reels are here.

Slow a concertina eddies
from Valencia crepe, jigs up
by bodrán to Apples in Winter.

Autonomic Stitch

Here on rug
as Cambridge field

        the script is open
        which is to   which is to
        let   all we've drawn   apart

          in lifetime halves
        here   and   there

    come
    point
    to curve

                feather touch
             firmer hug
          glaze-glance

    belong in poetic fit

Presliad

Rock-a-hula-hoop   willow twirled
      so glad you're
    here like hips to fingertips
love me tender buttons spinning
                  a little mixed up
but never   let me go
          as every beat
      lights the sky
    by barefoot
wonder
     no one else
       will weave
the pieces past   the flowers
              to neck
      for keeps
    so you play
   the keys
a simple charm   fever blonde
     come what may
       she's grace in place of Beale

Springsome

Hill strider
early beckoned each name has
of bird and plant
reading back
to Derbyshire frame
all a father's stock in motion
light pounded she roves on moor
with buzzard mew and fleeting deer.

Spry dancer
come courtly in red-black dress
to shine each strip
of floor and wall
she smiles a tropic note
Lowland pitched under burden
missing a mother's tonguespun care
still able to live as novel present starts.

Site lyrist
of stone and turf the foundling
weather divines
here to focus
point behind feature
like leats for the hungry gap
or banjo enclosure as chiefest table
she tells through dream a sampler tale.

Remate

Clever lines you may serve
when to say goodbye
means white sand
swirled and laid smooth
but you might more convey
a simple starting
in relief
now a face ungilt
draws give to desire
gently
as a press
on home-felt shore

from **Days of '49**

1997–1999

On the Slate

A for Attlee's American loan.
B for Bankside benefits.
C for Cripps riding a Comet.
D for Dobell's, damn devaluation.
E for Empire in Ealing's dream.
F for free specs, false teeth.
G for Goon Show with overstretch.
H for Homes on the Horizon.
I for ink as Into the Wind.
J for Jerusalem rising from ashes.
K for Kind Hearts and Coronets.
L for London rocket and Legal Aid.
M for make-do and mend.
N for NATO and Never Again.
O for Orange juice from the bottle.
P for Prescription, a shilling a go.
Q for the way to the Queen of Spades.
R for Rosehip syrup on the ration book.
S for Steel which takes the strain.
T for Tobacco, better than tools.
U for untreated smalls: Nutty Slack.
V for vesting day in a Vauxhall Velox.
W for welfare and a war won.
X for the ray to see down a tube.
Y for Yardley Lipstick lights.
Z for zither plucked in the Zone.

Red Light on Green

Play the music, open the cage
(catchphrase, *Variety Bandbox*)

Absolutely no Jokes about —
      Lavatories
      Effeminacy in men
      The Bible, e.g. 'B.C. (before Crosby)'
Suggestive references to —
      Ladies' underwear, e.g. winter draws on
      Animal habits, e.g. rabbits
      Lodgers
Sketches that might be taken to encourage —
      Strikes or industrial disputes
      Spivs and drones
Derogatory treatment of institutions, professions —
      'Cabinet requires the PM to doze'
      'A bishop's charge will include lightning devices'
      'Has any solicitor looked through her briefs?'
Remarks which endanger public safety —
      'One for the road'
      'Jump the electric current'
Expletives unfit for light entertainment —
      God, Good God, Blast, Damn, Gorblimey, ruddy etc.
Take extreme care over —
      Pre-natal influences ('His mother was frightened by
          a donkey')
      Marital infidelity
Avoid vulgar use of words such as 'basket' and any allusion
      to —
      'MacGillicuddy Reeks'
      'Lickey End, Worcs'
      'Muff Frontier Post'
Do not employ the terms —
      'Nigger' ('Nigger Minstrels' is allowed)
      'Chinamen'
Make all reasonable attempts to eliminate —
      Noisy advanced jazz, e.g. Stan Kenton, on a Sunday

Messages, e.g. a tune 'with love from Joan'
or 'it reminds me of happy hours with . . .'
Names of pubs or schools
Maintain alertness to titles —
No 'Get Up Those Stairs, Mademoiselle'
No 'Two Old Maids in a Folding Bed'
No 'Foggy Foggy Dew' (except by Benjamin Britten)
The choice of LP music should not be a left-handed version
of some other choice. Even in VARIETY
A tone is to be observed —
'Open the Door, Richard!' should not be sung in a drunken
    manner
'So Deep is the Night' may only be played as a straight ballad
Cut out the banter —
'I have one or two hobbies that Sir Stafford can't control'
'For us it was love at first hearing'
'In France nobody bats an eyelid'
Certain cross-references are permissible —
'When Sir Short Supply was in Tomtopia'
'There's Much Binding in the Marsh'
'Pa Glum says Take It From Here'
Special considerations for overseas broadcasts —
Jokes like 'enough to make a Maltese Cross' are of doubtful
    value
Radiogenic means Home & Family, the dial that glows.

(Private and Confidential)

ANALOGUE: Soviet jamming of BBC Russian Service begins 24
April.

Bird in France

Last unissued, Doctor Robert
springs it, a yard of alto
on the rim, spun
by scratchy retrieval —
weight billows, a potato, a stone
with eyes alive

salt in the groove
'la même chose'
sows a beat (story)
out of war

tracks across
Nowhere twice, 52nd Street
Hot House . . .

chur-cheep, jink-tzit
slides, slurs
sung in the grid
reedy-metallic

a continent latched on
to go over, for-mee-dar-ble
faces reflected in a bucket
(champagne on ice)

respect like the classics
for fingers, plump
tapering, and lips
above the suit

skin isn't the issue
even if spades lie up

steeped in the riff
and away, high and hard
night of the working
Five

Faust Variations

Terrible is the way you pronounce good. Mediocrity has no theological status. BREAKTHROUGH comes as the word unseen — vibrates — in a row on the Proving Ground. A little cut in the hand will release in a jar what fuels the stars. A pillar of purple fire, a mushroom seething in foam. With a brief soul-cry, wouldn't anybody want to keep ahead? Every maker carries within a canon of the forbidden, the self-forbidding, which includes all the possibilities. What does 'dead' mean when flora grows so rankly?

Lien in the dark with irksome mygrym, retching and spewing. To the sofa-corner comes my visitor with a white collar and a bow-tie. What troubles you? I am no flattering claw-back come to fetch you in. That rumour is learned gibberidge. Are you afraid of yourself? Plesure is yet yonge. There is time for it, plenteous, boundless time. A man may live at rack and manger like a lord. See the little neck through which the red sand runs in a threadlike trickle. Let us say XXIV years. But that is so far away, the narrow part, it is not worth thinking about.

Elsie Butler, who has dined with Crowley, finishes the third volume of her magical trilogy: Faust for the Goethe Year. It languishes in the basement of the C.U.P. offices. H.D. sees *Silver Wings* as a theft from life when all is coincidence. Old Crow is real but off-stage ('Do what thou wilt shall be the whole of the Law. I am the Magician and the Exorcist'). This contact out of the blue lays part of the floor for *Helen in Egypt*: did the events really occur and in what country? '[F]eeling and thinking as a real woman, she is but a shade, and one perhaps who has never had a real existence except in the minds of men' (*The Fortunes of Faust*). *Faust* is staged in the Open Air Theatre, Regent's Park with the final scenes from Part II (9th August).

PRIEST FREES MT. RAINIER BOY REPORTED HELD IN DEVIL'S GRIP — *The Washington Post*, 20th August. Ritual of Exorcism Repeated. Bed shakes violently at night with scratching or dripping noises from walls and mattress. Boy spouts Latin, a language he has never studied: 'O sacerdos Christi, tu scis me esse diabolum'. Spits into the face of priest while welts and stripes appear on his body. Blotched words, HELL, GO, X, and a bat-like devil. Brandings. Obscene talk and gestures, flung excreta. Slashes priest's arm from shoulder to wrist. EXIT appears on

Her touch burns on my cheek. O the allurements of ambiguity. To deal and dole the epithets of angel-talk: black-eyed Esmeralda, swan-necked Godeau. To be struck by this, I that have been love's whip. To feel such rays as shake off winter. Biron's monologue shows a miner in a dark shaft starkly pointing to the joy ahead. So remodel the earth. *Rosaline* says it's gravity's revolt, a firebloom which starts by mischief. With theatre in the blood one face bespeaks another, like Moon-gold. Out of number-magic you jump the chord obsolete. A merry gleam between the darkness of her lashes. Others don't think to look behind the curtain: pleats stirred by the breeze. I could vanish, she whispers, a dream now to myself.

Sweet Black Angel . . . Like the way she spreads her wings. No pallid Venus makes the stuff worthwhile. Legend: that itch to expose the unexposed, to see the unseen, the not-to-be and not-expecting-to-be-seen. Like kissing on another planet or through a quartz window on the ocean floor. Glissando. Just say the word. Whenever you call I'll come back—in *pulchra forma humana*. (There's a catch somewhere. You can't erase your signature.)

boy's chest, then he speaks: 'I am St Michael. I command you, Satan and other spirits, to leave this body. Now.' Symptoms vanish. Priest asks for a sign—gunshot echoes through hallway. Boy's aunt was a medium. Physics prof. says there is much we have yet to discover about electro-magnetism.

A miracle of unification of a nation (or what is left of it) is achieved when on 28th August, in American occupied Frankfort-on-Main, all parties, inclusive of Communists, pay homage to the memory of Germany's greatest son. 'It takes a whole life to know Goethe thoroughly—but a year is too much' says Erich Kästner of *Emil and the Detectives*.

Analysis following a B-52 flight shows that the Soviet Union has exploded its first atomic bomb. President Truman announces this to the American people on 23rd September. The People's Republic of China is proclaimed on the 1st October. Stalin is 70 years old and stifling from emptiness and loneliness. Partly in response to 'Joe I', the GAC of the Atomic Energy Commission, chaired by J. Robert Oppenheimer, states that it would be ethically wrong to develop the H-bomb. This advice is overruled.

The town council of Marktredwitz resolves that a street named after the writer Thomas Mann should be renamed Goethestraße. A spokesman says that since the war Mann has behaved with a lack of piety towards

To empty a sack of gold and find only sand is the grim deposit of saga. Liars & lickspittles mixed us a poison draught, there in the Cococello Club or the great Nike room. Riddle me in a Zip-pan like the debauch on exchange. How the time reeked of beauty, and now this whole history is refuted. Clung round by demons, a hand over one eye, our marble statue descends to Avernus lighted by the dance of the roaring flames. 'Nuff' he cries, still staved in a G-e-r-m-a-n performance.

A piece of gold can make you see different. Now every habit and remark tips toward parody. The sentence is scraps stolen from a feast. Mayhap he did but delude me, that other, a wily-pie. It's never too late. Looks like some make-bate burning the bond if Hell is we ourselves. ZOLO GO pauses the bluff on a barrel organ.

Magic is music: 'an unfit study for any person who is prey to the reproaches of memory' (P.B. Shelley). Blue-pencilled by the rhymester, a marginal note is not so marginal. The flying messenger wants guidance and here everything leaves off.

his fatherland. He is blatantly devoid of true inner culture [Herzensbildung]. Few copies of Doktor Faustus are available in Germany. By these windings and vaultings any note can be sharpened or flattened.

Freeman J. Dyson enrolls as one of Hans Bethe's graduate students at Cornell University. (Four years later Thomas Pynchon studies Engineering Physics.) The bunch of weaponeers includes many Los Alamos physicists. 'I'll be damned if I'll let anybody in Washington or any politicians tell me what work not to do,' says Norris Bradbury, Director of Los Alamos.

Elsie Butler delivers a lecture on Byron and Goethe: 'seeking and never finding each other, and yet (half-obsessed the one, wholly obsessed the other) aware of a strange affinity'. Byron's Cain is produced by the Rudolf Steiner School of Dramatic Art with the second act omitted. 'Faustish'. What if MacNeice were propelled to write a Goethean line or two, snuffed in the radio tower? He grips a Guinness at the bend of the bar, refuses to look at Shelley ('slipshod and not much of a poet'). A Faust goes out in six parts, October/November.

René Clair's La Beauté du Diable is filmed in Rome. He refers to Heine's comment: 'Every man should write a Faust.' Mephisto is the common man— grumbling, greedy, a figure of farce. Vanquished by his own devices, he disappears in a column of smoke.

Noir

A stem of light rooting
for the story that's never
going to work. Say, Laurie & Bart
who's come from Rope. Out west
it's always one last job
in the asphalt. A shop, a bank,
a meatpacking plant, with blocked-out seizures
on the road, the stars in limbo.
A language tunnelled beneath
the production code, a zigzag fuse
leading anywhere but, *détourned*
to have it all. Together
like guns & ammunition
kiss-driven
he can't control the breakneck
deviousness of the plot
that's caught faster
in a shrinking frame
with the yelp of dogs. Into bed
and into trouble, high-grain
on a deadly roost as if
none of it really happened.
Corrosion or a name scratched out.
Better the shrouded peak with no other record
soul-pacted.
She dreams they're walking
in a forest and he's pinned
by steel. She is fatal
from low angle, she's taken
the job, the home, she's
not going to settle
for a life of as you were.
Honour smoulders like a tacked-on finish.
Say the word often enough
and it's just a sound
shockproof. He's another tool
in the dust, the heat

subtracted to a mask:
she's after something else.
Beer, rum, lemon soda.
Does anything mix? Midnight French
is a slippery term the year after
Artaud. From bomber to bar
she's got that ballad smoke
rehearsed from the heart. 'Situation Wanted'
if he can hold a snake, she's going
with the Voice, criss-cross
(all bubble bath and moonlight
and inside blue steel).
Flying in the sky outspread
it got wilder and hazier.
From the flares to the fiesta
you don't know what to fight.
A fixer with sore feet. Back to this
the bigger the bomb the quicker —
let it go, rebop war abandon
to sturdy strivers. Murder happens
between the shade and the window sill
slatted between shortage and renewal.
A black hole in the sunlight
stairs destroyed to the third floor.
Suspicion spreads by a glance, a pause
like someone else's riddle.
The dark answer is
it's for no reason, no reason at all.
Who's listing behind the spot
puts they's living
on the line, a caustic crack.
Second person told
you're out of the party
and you're guilty —
guilty & innocent
there's nothing between.

Four Star Puzzle

RKO, 7.7.49
(after Anthony Mann and Lillie Hayward)

Follow me quietly
at night—
high heels on a wet pavement.

She's come to interfere.

Follow me quietly
till the set is complete—
just add these facts together.

Who's the Judge, the last grip?

Follow me quietly
to the office—
blank-face in a chair.

Off-angle he's brought the vital piece.

Follow me quietly
up the catwalk—
splashing pipes, catch and let go.

A true crime rookie she gets her man.

ManU/Mersenne Primer

I tries to store ◀▶ in one-ton spread
your subject flicker ◁▷ goodless godless
I spy I ply ◀▶ first letter cueing
down drum and tube ◁▷ bit by bit
are these ◀▶ mansion dolls
are these ◁▷ berry cobbles
I almost sense ◀▶ can certainly scan
whatever you give ◁▷ put in put out
on paper-tape ◀▶ gone from Baby
to MADM ◁▷ all of thirty-six miles
tome-space approx. ◀▶ to test and find
factrobble digits ◁▷ a wiry little system
flashes through the murk ◀▶ no addlepate
no onionskin ◁▷ just d-d-dyou want
halcyon wrybates ◀▶ rotable purlieu
tropological hairness ◁▷ ouzled shirtcut
horrorskip meddler ◀▶ these or any
seamed to order ◁▷ I ken I con
under metal plates and rods ◀▶ groping
the far-domed landscape ◁▷ will draw
a new idea for the old shambles ◀▶ boil
this turf, timber to wage-stop ◁▷ ever
patient as last tram leaves ◀▶ tighten
or spill might one day ◁▷ usable
save me you me you ◀▶ so implies
that turinigma ◁▷ if I if it could perform
capricious ◀▶ leaking to remind
and fit ◁▷ the special rumnant need
inkle alpha edzo ◀▶ my engine free
to attune and be held ◁▷ then would be
blood, gaze and gesture ◀▶ woken indeed

A Line Engraved

for Frances

riff-raff step out
on the trail
placarded off
or founderously
barbed

Dalton and de Freitas
the Castles
take back
with tousled hair
and knapsack

the green-ribbed
preserve
that peoples
itself

disclosing
the small
other
din
of moorlark
and stream

the white or purple
flower
beyond scathed branches

The Small Back Room

Now when I direct a black-and-white film . . . I don't give a damn
about the audience. I only care about the camera and me—I am the
audience and the camera is me. Do you see?   —Michael Powell

What's a woman like you doing,
a prop to his growl against
the world? What's in the story
of a tin foot, a bottle and a bomb
when things are on the mend? What's
the point of seeing it
shingly or shuttered
like love through the keyhole?

There's a small boy inside
with a lighted match. It's
a personal matter, going with
a clamp and a wrench
to get at the heart.

He sits out the dance
at the Hickory Tree. She's tough
for once with luminous eyes
and rips her picture
from the frame he'll smash.

Whirling, whistling, Time
makes the whisky grow
to a giant. You can keep
your gut-rot, Sammy, prompt-proof
as the telephone rings.

What makes it tick, upright
in pebbles that shift,
delicate on a bank that curves
thin as the new moon? Three to one
it's this way in. Any takers?

Nearer and nearer briefed
his fingers on the screws:
a slip would repeat
the dance with death
as a special matinée.

Seventeen minutes is the same
as the ballet, the longest
an audience will hold its breath.
Sue's a number to call
in case of misadventure.

Mopped off, he stares at a thermos
with a black cap. (Too much scotch —
could do with one now.) Undone
there's a simple trembler tongue
between terminals, and a second.

All over, he's a quiet hero
who may not always take
with (quote) both hands. She comes
from the shadows, this time
barely, a move ahead.

Life's in the corner of his smile
reaching across or letting
Narcissus die. The wait
has lifted, war-wise,
a lid of longing that can't.

One would like to forget one would
like to remember the devil
with another face, a night
of swing away from home.
Close-up, with the name Byron
she's a lynx who'd dare
slip the spirit
to any worth his salt.

Bacon Heads

in space **alone** a mouth screams
leathery

from blitzed satin

in one **fix** or another

unnamable graft
ergot stubble

gibbers to be

zinc on furls

can't be dodged

snout of all pomp

ar**raigned** with a tassle

under the case: eclipse

Francis Bacon, **Heads I-VI**
Hanover Gallery, 8 November–10 December

Stromboli

CAN'T HEAR (the water churning)
CAN'T UNDERSTAND (the boarded door)
CAN'T SPEAK (the smoking cone)
ARRIVE ROME SUNDAY NIGHT (fiesta)
foreign as a kiss through barbed wire.
Our first lady of the screen, NUN BELOVED
walks over investment, her soul on a hero's belt.
Gone with a love pirate, that Italian in a red car
sends fire and ashes to the Legion of Decency.

SCENT *AMORE* in lines on a matchbox
picture with no script, shower or wardrobe.
You wait for the person who makes you leave.
A BETRAYAL OF THE GLOSS FOR ORDINARY PEOPLE.
Start of film. Blank. Try to start. Fault. Start.
Vene, this is *bad* room. We plant again—barley, vines.
Leave me alone (gripping the iron headboard):
I'm different. From another world.

Out of black rock comes sparta grass.
Karin chews a sprig, brushes it against her cheek.
Hangs a curtain up, has the legs of the chairs
cut shorter, paints flowers on the wall.
And the hooded faces stare: You ave-a no modesty.
Who understands the space of a woman?
She's a rabbit seized by a ferret, she's a tunny fish
speared in the heaving sea. She can charm
the lighthouse keeper in a cave. She starts
the sulphur flow in her kitchen.
BABY DUE SHOCKS FILMDOM.

She puts on her dress to climb over the mountain
marked with mouths or eyes.
Up to the black gullet, the crimson lip
which belches. Suitcase, purse, money
fall away, with her wedding ring in close-up.
Coughs and cries in a haze. Enough, enough

I can't go back. SEVEN YEARS in a long shot.
NO ALIEN GUILTY CAN SET FOOT
ON AMERICAN SOIL. But the mystery, the beauty
when you wake, gulls wheeling overhead.

An ending is imagined: return or escape?
The backer MR HUGHES chops for a headline
but writes to defend the heart: REALITY IS
A MATTER OF INTENT. In the finish it begins again.

Diagonal

I begins bare from a point — shall you be named —
in the wake of ruins: the mother-stamp
de la Lee or atte Lee, the father salt
like saddlery. She comes from fire service
hooded in a siren suit. He comes burst
from a Sherwood turret, ranging again
to write left-handed. To build home
they route-plot through dreams of silver on magenta:
a place at Haileybury at six months. Oxford and the Law.
The severity of the razor-edge with overlapping mudguards.

Sleep in a pram in the front garden
when nobody would carry one off. Crawl backwards
over ink dots, dizzy-reliant. Toddle to the zoo
to meet a snake or, gothic-idoled, stare in awe
at dinosaurs and whales. Stuff twigs
down the plughole, stand at Jason's helm
drifting in the tunnel, breathe the smoke
of the Great Western, laugh to death
at Captain Hook, get stuck on rhyme
told nightly at Flores in the Azores.

Roy Rogers meets Robin Hood
meets Ivanhoe on the new screen
with hours rationed. It's a safe world
shadowed by rockets. Run in the V
of Muddy Lane pushed by Himmel Hyatt,
learn the collect or be beaten as the sum
adds up. He plucks I Only Want
To Be With You, kissing Dusty in the garage.
What were you doing when the president
was shot — seen with a hundred variations?

Seven daffodils sing the Mojos, a dandy on the tiles
steamhammer dancing to Long John and Rod
frills on his chest and a tab-down collar
steps later and later in the basement

on rum n'coke as all the girls chorus
to a wall of amps and the lights go pink
like Waterloo Sunset. Last train gone
it's get your rocks off, touches is so
and the portrait gives, fur parting
in a starry gasp. Next heave

the pentameter in Grosvenor Square, scared violins
prompt their odyssey, one small step
on a bawdy planet. She trips in gingham
to his green satin, stealing through a guru gatefold:
White Rabbit, White Album, White Wonder.
Teeth on the strings, whose mask is too much
for the mirror? Anyone almost pulls through
when the Hessian choice isn't a single thread.
Albion lies beneath a suckling tree
which projects the Wicker Man.

Blacked out with no oil
at a quarter century it's the end of gold.
Leyland mounts the tug of the heavies
to bite the hand. Glam turns to punk
as a shadow overtakes. We're at work
locked in Troytown, mazily coursing
the heath on Sunday. Rid of flares
you can pencil flesh, playing a forbidden
tune. She knocks at the door, says I'm yours
two nights a week.

Angel eyes is the other side of Iron
reaping what was sown, the P.M. declares
dumping a dream as must, her coach and horses
driven by the throat of a rising loan.
There's an end to double fantasy
in the Dakota Hotel. Irreversibly fooled
with a rhythm stick, anyone can do it
still has a buzz or an edge.
A cruiser sunk aghast with flags
warms the vote to extend

Less-than-life. Who's not complicit
Coal not dole cries in a bucket
for indie suits sharp under neon
are the same advert for the private run.
And we meet on the floor ecstatic. She's ripened
into Venus with a Liberty dress. Newsprint rolls
an electric fix, growing as the self recedes.
Pitched by the promise to own
he has sheets to nestle her ache
to belong in a different tense.

High Edwardian with a rose-girdle, cats by the fire
fill a void as the thump strikes and you step
into your father's shoes. Wielding the word
again one's ready to share: cream grilled salmon
in a line of peppers with white Burgundy.
Hands clasped through each reel to the drive
and quilt talk. She flashes blue eyes in a Latin storm
catching his laughter in a pyramid at noon, friends
walking east when the wall is down, one
bloated as a box on the sea.

A second hammer and a third marks the end
it seems with shivering glass. Salt my element rubs
ruddy night, chartered, pepped and themed
as only a wine-mate on the companion-way
can see. Kin thickens to guide a son, a brother, in return.
Out of the round you enter without a talking heart
Mayday spins a revamp, some limbs in the cabinet stir.
She's not a people's princess stayed in the underpass
or a seagull thrashing under the dome. Yet one flick
can coax a nineties number to a five-spot cheer.

Uncollected

1999–2001

Cromer Contours

In
  her
    lemon
      suit
      she
    smiles
  across
the
  sand
    almond
      eyes
      alert
    and
  dreamy
over
  ribs
    moist
      to
      touch
    and
  warm
with
  prospect
    of
      cliff
      or
    pier
  tonic
that
  starts
    again
      like
      crabs
    castles
  their
sovenance

Swimmer's Wake: 4 Nashscapes

In both places I was nearly drowned . . . [by]
spring or winter seas.

Paul Nash, *Outline* (1949)

Stone, wood, iron
waves
heave and curl

> crash against
> outcrop pyramids
> rattled
> at the join

>> a triquet splayed
>> to try
>> the sousing spirit

who approaches
in the lighthouse beam   a path of plates
on a cliff to the north   blades or folds
in December   back to the skyline
its edge a zig-zag tear   bitter and beguiling
draws

> this eye
> the field
> of lash and buffet
> to rest
> as birds
> go down
> a flake mere
> re-plied
> in wonder strike

Vortex Rerun

More then the rock amyddys ye raging seas
The constant heart no danger dreaddys nor fearys

Rising from water fury that might be
a womb of leather or fur, the triton
captain tries to punch out Peace, who,
calm in a black-rimmed quarter-segment,
strokes his arm, as in the moment beside
(or behind) a ship founders, mainmast broken
over crew leaping to boats. The face of a corpse
ruffed in surf floats between rock and skiff,
pointing a way perhaps to land. Brother
of a hero, he'll inherit for a spell
after the sweating takes that voyager
come through wrack and confinement
to a glorious rest drawn in the sky
or surrender worse than a storm.

H[ans] E[worth], *Sir John Luttrell* (1550/91)
Courtauld Institute/Dunster Castle

from **Le Fanu's Ghost**

2001–2006

Tomogram

for Glenn Storhaug

Your text is the ghost of a call
(I did not ring)
but since after all the message
yields up

> Caxton's **H**
> a panel of ink starvation
> as seen in Gothic — 'gastly for to see'

the word is as much as breath
at three removes

> beyond the jurisdiction of veracity
> paling in a spectral line

nobody's flicker, that screen double
who crosses your brain

> misread and so enshrined
> the train outside the table

darts fire, do you mind that mark
out of a cutting

> Vindicta's special agent
> clangs a silent bell

plaze ax what's the bother —
the blankets tossed about

> stealing, don't you tell on me
> back to some fac simile

a tuft of ivy in place of the face
nodding

quit-rent
to feed the rollers

with even dirt   an island
stark from the press

amarantus albus
a cell deprived
a white coal

for vault-age there's this
demand

OVER the over
and stifling why

freaked into touch
to be passing honest

your putative reader
starts

when wages walk or another
writes my dispatches
I entertain the jest in the geist
and turn things to account

Burnt Custom, Bright Shroud

Cranes over the Liffey
their concrete bags suspended

groan and quiver to pile great layers
once like marble out of mud

the bus stop is mute on Lower Abbey Street
no diehard tumbler's grace

crouching dragon, leaping tiger
grills the time in digi-frame

get big, get niche or get out
who picks banjo from the Confession Box

Georgian storeys lean on steel
lady Gaunt dressed in polythene

land skip services paint me a sign
Founded Not Long Ago

rhubarb on the railings
says someone was here

spots of rain disperse my words

Glass Master

Launder the notes
and push your business
       sideways
       a lost radio show
       like Spenser sang it

Limb, limn Limerick
(what is ever over)
play us a bit of a tune

out of every corner
lichen and moss
knotted oak
silver shafts of birch
something of the real right feeling
speaks

       a shriek beneath
       the stones
       a bally vision
       with the sense
       half-broke

spin for tonight only
fast aflutter slowed
the cry that cries to cry
one heart one tongue one ground
when the fork is driven deep

       there they all come in
       tag and rag
       an undertaker planted West
       makes a word razed out
       ourselves alone

who's skulking behind hedges
auditors will testify

thirty miles as the crow
to Hap Hazard

      rakehelly horseboys
      without a name
      kern and gallowglass
      shaggy and jagged

harpers or rhymers
with sweet bait
glibbed to render
the tryst after death
on wasteful hills

a taste of New Edge
filtered by incense
fashions a ditty into a dagger
for Irene's good knight
to revive

      the face on the back
      is your self or your friend
      there to rehearse
      at feasts and meetings
      how things began or mean
      to go on

Whiteboys and Oakboys
blank each loaded purpose
to pick out of the soil
a living

      gusty stinky belchy
      loose-gobbed slop-mouthed
      bag-bellied folk
      will bash and batter

through the keep on the cliff
through the choir
that's forfeit

do you hear the Mary
in Maritime the M
in Monarch as iron-struck
that letter drops

no rent and no tithes
this message don't fade way
backed by the blaze of lead

Shame us by scoring the faces of saints
pulling pitiless the rood
to let all charring pages go
from an altar stain

loop the days and this track
is Captain Rock
tramping the wood by moonlight
to get some echo back

Broadwater is Blackwater
blood running placid
to the sea

your seam-text is Death without the priest
whether the bombed admiral
does like the abbey roast
by subdearfugue or skeltershute
he lies with squelching feet
skull shattered like a gourd

down the road
has no middle
squaddies clank metallic
prod the shins
over bottles and stones

a rifle butt is nervous
bangs a crucifix or little virgin
to get at truth
behind burning bars

open coat hands on head
what's the name where
you going

cake the walls with a kind of mud
(why say helpless) as the blatant beast
in a key-cold embrace
blankets one stark hide

tit for tat
under the hood
there's a hum
made white
in bits and bites

servant to master child to mother
shuttle the crystal
by code

a dragonfly
down pits burnt away
or graven loughs
shoulder to shoulder

here we go round
the dates et cetera
you say one I say naught
can shift the mark
on a devil's piece

to get level
the right hand clutches
a lock of hair
as the beam overreached
tumbles

read the rings of the mirror
gyral where all the world is caught

> will you come will you will you
> come to the bower

a short story — cut long

> and sure it is still so sweet
> a glen with a brawling stream
> in leafy coils

each chip carries the scene across
first come tragic then gone farce

> this is the bull
> taken as blunder
> that tells hub to rim
> what reckoning
> beckons

in either version of Ardour
won at the track or the table
what You did I must suffer

> there in the malt
> stamped on a sheet
> slicer answers server

Braced Planes

This is the oak which frames the room

This is the picture that mirrors the line

This is the glass that offers a prospect

This is the fire which draws you round

This is the stair which climbs like ivy

This is the key which makes all secure

This is the loan that makes it a shadow

This is the bond that makes it right

This is the bill just got at the table

This is the helper who deals you a smash

Faded Novel: Fine Again

Is blake ladder a 𝖉𝖊𝖆𝖉 ladder? spriks another longwedge De oud huis bij de kerkegaard (high fen ate it) as mite Schalken up at the loftleaved elm phone attic foenix true the ears — fizz seben dean sex tea seben — as won cullbrit knot by know mins a fee neon throbs a knockout. Some you'll beak it say he'd reverse the wards: spectacles silver thee of knight, smoke narcotic white, rising ghost a like, dagger outdrew. By rackrent quirks a pro-licks cartoon uncalls all wor[l]ds atouched under stone and branch in outpoised doublin': here's how to haul iffy cross chat factor fib, a poplar witness all we ever saw to be a bout two — I's gone still make out a winnerful livaccord to shame us choice. Arnheim lost bobs up our gain in a dribble-ticker, value'm tree: **arc, arch, archer**. Strikes turk the face without a date damns pacific, as Lefanunian the barracked R.I.A. was where ironhead casts a bosky shadow in Bodger's Wode. A dry leaf is a banner, awethor's print of a clodded shoesole, a finger-sion, a volant touch, a ledged crime invincible cut. Watt underlays the zod? doz. the **e** chain too the **f** and how do you right that **F**? Catch yore Tartar in daungierfelt. Dare gores sum body living/dead — neither one nor t'other quite — a vampire scrambles across clusters MIRCALLA ➔

CARMILLA ➜   **MILLARCA** push the
M out to the margin. Earland fires her cousin.
Would the wad maid flash trink a trink upstares,
draft move in treeum dime? Unchain jed under
de-sign diss awl mucks room for castlemallards
nutter. Goes trite a pair a-gruff, darn high eight
[re]us in **MS**: krik krak. Found le cure — is it in
airnest, blew shot wit read? A runsucked text
is May tricks. You's like the river, Miss is chap
[h]ell just desert (it's odd). She fixes her I's,
Eyesalt, on the gonne Treestone: Mildew Lisa
how he smiles in the bow surge, the ring, uni-
ball hive of breath — to underneat proise releaf
by zolo kuei-ver. Trick **L** of fey tall footnote
(mansioned a four) ♫ ♫ in ah tic you low more
'tis calls the blackwarder. *Poithon* or *Pison* the
voyeurwaker said he had after that dizzy dish
of chat, be-Sherrydaned to walk in proargrease.
Dan pixillated does leary deeds in the Horndead
Inkbattle. Hour dark dayed retrospectioner
wrytreats into iz own claybook and gives you a
turn is itself about

Casement

Could not be called a cave. Dark and bright the stones.
United by labour. A vaulted passage with many stairs.
Reft of reach. Sunbeams strain through painted glass.
Friend is the voice carried by holes in a statue. Family
covers forbidden issue. Echoes with the lightest foot.
A song can dilate the heart while passion still is hid.

Black velvet den
under azure seal
winding wormly
away from what
is fled the world.
Half hallowed to
reflower. Ghouls
slip between self
and relation, she
goes ruin strewn
to the summons
(such a guardian
as wolf to lamb).
Why style a safe
home a prison?

Can't get out and
if you do there is
another version.
Appear singular
as story fractures
rambling against
fact. White turns
to cream — week,
month, year. All
figments partake
of tunnelled ore:
cyphers, sonnets,
ringlets of hair.
Whether to skirt
no is our refrain.

Must our hearts throb before inanimate canvas? Who
in a castle was kept a princely guest like jewels secure.
The door so often sought is that portrait deftly sprung
in the flickering murk. Seen without being known as
lost and when marked ready to vent this space. Again
letters betray. Residua cleave to the rendered casket.

Bacon Dust

FACT

leaves

its

ghost

a sp-a-sm in the moment

still   the figure *volante*

a small black monkey

eyes poked   teeth grinning

walks over **Rembrandt**

waits for the slot

a beautiful cut

three there were three of us

leaning stalks

clone-spill

from a can of butter beans

in sky-lit **Kensington**

yo-tinks brought back

to trash out gilt

like a **DAZ** carton upended

the Pope of Lower Baggot street

Speedwell

Billy bright eye blue at wayside stares
a white core in touch-me I'll break
basin
       dotherum botherum
                      sewn
on clothes a sprig to keep from harm

comes creeping to shriek goodbye
could pick yours too — by strike-fire

gives you his heart his face
in a handkerchief caught
                   this splash
of spring

𝕸änner 𝕿reue what is it
froliclavish drool
           or stalklong
                  strut
in quink-stained heaven

don't disremember the spell
draws a leaf from the ground —

darling lie with me on grass
or hedge-bank
          petals fused
            so five makes four
will last as long as held

cat's eye/lark's eye/lady's thimble
deep at wood's edge
cluster
      prompt pulseful
                tread
(to fear an acre is never to go)

Chaocipher

```
allgo   spell   light   house   style
under   stand   still   frame   uprip
eerie   r-ish   dance   death   watch
pulse   comes   musky   along   alley
smoke   while   split   words   argue
whose   black   quill   caput   pours
awake   lyric   about   river   broad
swift   beats   again   skull   could
drape   moore   edges   green   among
metro   polis   wilde   loves   salon
trial   after   rhyme   yeats   takes
glass   golem   blind   going   joyce
canco   nnect   ionbe   tween   thema
ndthe   prosp   ectai   sling   orimm
rambe   disco   vered   hidin   gamor
tifer   laugh   insen   chaid   craft
qyslt   gigfn   raudd   exzuz   oblal
tates   halov   xcutt   ortio   isact
squse   filbo   mquin   dxrly   lhugs
tdbit   naary   kisde   sovdh   luyre
pumpa   zevlt   ellum   lipsl   jeozi
rltys   raibl   eirsa   scgom   errho
hming   vozzi   ovinc   eworl   shaow
pictd   zlant   orcos   brrny   yares
```

Liberty Knots

A white cross on the door
is always there
wherever you go

across the cobbled street
under a high wall
over rolling water

See me safe
I'm looking behind
someone's pointing
a pistol or dagger

How should I have gold —
I am a scholar

whose words turn
in the devil's setting

'sacred' for 'scared'
'breath' for 'breach'
'stay' for 'slay'

A victim gets his plot
on the bones of another —
stare in his face, it's you
here but for stony grace

Exquisite Corpse
Corpse Exquisite

I lay my length in the box
    to sleep a whole revolution of Saturn
whose lid slides across, inches above
    a few light words only in sport
crunch home the screws
    for ever eyes closed bright
and still viewing
    syrup infused in wine
 a study in *mortis imago*

I have my beloved *souvenir*
    a rose-bud to my heart
but this is the violation of letters
    of what man is capable
too tremblingly pressed
    by wildest wishes
to supply a connected narrative
    (take, take back the gift
I conversed but with a costume)

Are we any wiser as we grow
    disburthened of gauze and torches
or is it our illusions which change
    one single object in steel or taffety
like your skeleton-key, I see the ceiling
    burnished to prove
what no chemistry can detect
    in four times so many years
tried by a terrible escape

Duelling Tales

Did he the villain dag her, did he
Captain or Major Mathews
put his hand on her knee, the prettiest
creature stripped you ever saw

Did she mix poison with pain powder
did she ask Dick to play the knight
did she make plans with both
to go off, her portrait incomplete

Did the protector play the lover
turn Eliza's convent to a wedding
vow, so to be posted in the Bath paper
a L[iar] and a S[coundrel]

Did Mr S go to Mr M at Crutched Friars
where the key was lost and he still
got in, did he who had sworn his death
call him dear friend and cry off the fight

Did they meet in a tavern by candlelight
did M beg for his life but refuse to sign
and then on the point retract
while Eliza knows her man

Did they each a hero set out the fact
did they meet on Kingsdown to decide
again, jab and stab till her locket breaks
and one rush off with the other 'dying'

Did she sing that day, the only person
not to know, did he do it for the name
of Gentleman, to keep a Maid may-be
none the less a nightingale

Riddle

A man is made of two embraces
tingle the top, tie the toe

a Linnet sings, an Owl stitches
silk in the morning blab at night

if all the notes were lime and smoke
attachment would be inside-out

dare drink this to run away
chestnut hair, then green eyes

house of motion, house of sleep
here's the moment but it's not

blazing comet in a Venice glass
he's SHERI to one, to the other DAN

Polesden Lacey

Against the brink of war, of debt
Dan buys his sweet, Hecca
the place best within reach of Town
on the prime and sporting Downs

        you'll chirp like a bird
        bound like a fawn
        grow fat as little pig

the servants rid, we'll have all good
and do all good around

there is a peaceful valley, whatever
the boom of iron

        got from Admiral G—
        with the sale of Drury shares
        furniture in hock
        and a lawyer's loan (Geary's own)

honour bright, borrow and fear not
with a hatful of violets on the table
and three samples of lamb's wool

walk the terrace, slow, take in
this steep wooded bank
whose end is a peep
of lovely distance

        ha-ha drop
                south to the wild
        rabbits and deer
                cross vaulted track
        and up, trees wrapped
                in shadow
        Ranmore that no squire
                will enclose

my dear bit of brown Holland
come into the garden, I would like
my roses to see you

the Iliad even is a moonlit urn
by shag-headed beeches
that catch the wind
from the east

what if we don't go to church
we'll dine on claret
with not a candle to show
the way to bed

if breakfast sighs neglect
this is not a butter county

without you Dan is Lemoncholy
as a yew-tree in a church yard

Hogden, Connicut, Tanners Hatch
yield the poles to fence
and still both houses call
I want a speech on wood and canvas

Mick shall have plenty of matter
to go with tomorrow

No George — no war
No Pitt — no war

the throne we honour is the PEOPLE'S CHOICE
in cryptic Peru

riot is sown by wicked men
and who are they * * * * * * * * *
panders of a coney's will
get up the same old drama
with props and such, a little modernized

for natives to bite, a crown *con-spirito*
with lines alleged burning
metal into eye-cases
that make not meet a faction
in what cist-ear land are they
when it comes to trial

war-jaw haw-haw law-more
have-his-body-he-can't
brooding nightmare faces
in the trumpet's blare, the prickly bush
oily with a grin so decent
create the passions you persecute

From Nun's Walk these footsteps
are traceable like spots on a coat

dare d*ct*te what's bespoke under cover
there are many dark actors playing games

Erose

I

crossed hands in a box

brush against glass

avid absence

parts

squirrel fur

II

a glove dropped
(Lise's)

did you fling her
into the water

III

phrases at the frame
clasp a likeness
never seen

head in her lap, fingers
who's touched me
the hot frolic

IV

smile of the gaze-lady
gagged with a velvet band

it's a question of whether
you can fix a title

foolish to ask
what's there of meaning
it's the hint
of a stronger perfume

V

is that the forest
black beneath the lough
columns of marble
billowy clouds
the shaft of a dagger in satin

star bones splay
as a clock dissolved
crimson on ivory
be in me some
late admission of crime

five petals tremor
in the hazard of a moment
linked across borders
as the spume on the rib suggests
the final stroke on a rhyme

Alphacrux

		art	act		
		blend	brand		
		contend	consent		
		dame	damn		
		ergot	regret		
		fairies	furies		
		guard	guide		
		halcyon	helicon		
impudent	joyces	musted	misled	kindred	last
impotent	joists	noting	nothing	hundred	lust
		oak	rock		
		poison	prison		
		quiet	quite		
		reach	retch		
		soul	seal		
		truant	taunt		
		umbral	muddle		
		voice	vice		
		wave	wane		
		xerafin	seraphim		
		yours	years		
		zoom	zone		

Bootmarks and Fingersigns

Now come back like a truant, seeing plain. Through
the wicket from damp grass and hanging oak, into the lap
where the river winds blueish in a long brown stain
cut by slither-land. On Martin's Row the Tap
or the Villager talks olderwise: sepia chimneys
give us flax on the bed or stilled barley in a quarter cask
as barrack boys tread the lyric out. A framed article
stacks these moments in a floating present. Turn
to get the current gossip, bite a sandwich. There
on the glass there might be a signature. Or is that
a scratch on the table, a posted confession? Sip the rest
of a dark beverage, user over quota. Spa water comes
from a supermarket, a car hovers while the gate answers
its pulse code. Over at Izod's chapel, slit-windows
stand ready for siege: a white tower projects
what's hidden below. Tattered velvet may cover
staves of vanished flesh but who would stray
down steps that fade. Better rendered in air
a cross is draped with ivy and fallen, broken slabs
keep kindly counsel. A little mermaid in a circle
invokes the flood beneath (whispers hush-sh-sh-sh)
by body bent grace. All spells a far-off alarm in quiet
behind a wall shut from Phoenix great slopes, a plot
overtaken by nettles and dandelions. Warden, don't let
the lock bang fast, even raincloaked by willow or yew.

motocrime
u   l
l   a
t   g
i
r   r
d   o
a   l

microtome

Exercise for Ear

Lucy let the light in, through dreary hours
of winter

> Looe-see Looe-see
> follow your heart
> *chimerical*

down to hell-o-ease

> like the low notes
> of a rich-toned
> organ

that spirit-chamber

> wants which man
> out of glass will not
> go dull

might tug might lean

> a half-bound volume
> against your ruffled
> net-work

Silvine Memo

Long traced   this golden day   upcome
at the blue face   of the clock   we stop

a van sweeps by   we gulp   water
return to   walking   pace

all flesh   is grass   we eat
by   a gravestone   oak curtain

By Rule and Order of the Bellferry
Take off your Hat, Coat, Spurs

This Year Brother Broke/Then I first awoke
Rang a good Peal/For Framptons Weal

slab slides back   steps down   to the vault
a quiet bit   of theatre   with no
distinction   of   tenses

rock-set   'The Home' is   almshouses
their initials intertwined   of lovers eloped
M[arcia] M/R B[rinsley] s

the road   is straightened   out
the green door   is gone
even   the Squire's wall
that made   a better view
southside   than (burnt) cottages

the river   swift flowing   *Frome*
settled round   for fish   fine soil
idles   under   three arches
balustraded   with   Portland
a crusting motley
yellow   black   white

winds   and   wanders
knotweed   weir   rushes
watermeadows   osiers

cattle graze   easy   in lowland
pasture   the flick   of a tail
all that   taxes   content

the mansion is not there   **death dues** (1931)
four rows of windows   a double staircase
disperse   by a vanishing trick

> fatalities   of family   and place
> quiz   sidelong   the mould
> erected   only to   translate
> vain excess   or   radiant pile

a carriage drives up the gravel
to peacock cries   a fountain splash
by the great door   dreams 'Salve'
for a Lady   denied her children

a poet must gather poets
hidden   with   stock news
in the County Chronicle

vo'k a-gone   with zilver thread
trees in rank   along a ledge
do show   Victorianly
the parts   made over

a ghost-girl   rides   from Max Gate
startled   by a train
while here   at the table
from Algy's daughter
he wants to hear   'How oft Louisa'

cedars of Lebanon   stand proud
the Court   is   just
stable block   and   laundry

skeleton of a squeezed elite

broken and sold   piecemeal
over a decade
hall   saloon   gallery
shipped to America
mullions and lesser stone
put into the road to Sydling St Nicholas

free passage   for   butler and housemaid
neither flattered   nor   otherwise
on   Hog Cliff Hill

the footpaths are marked to Lanchard's
Plantation and Compton Valence
draft of a mosaic   laid   across

close-ruled lines   a stream
to serve   on stilts
every rood   of   ground

Criss Cross: In Irving's Shadow

Dub
me Pan
I'd rather
see a wood
bluebell-misty
than dress to the
gong in a mansion
to be vampired by silk
got at mixum-gatherum
when the moon makes her
own come sighing humming
as twins on walls and windows
a rustle a scratch on the armour of
settled rank elsewhere and otherwise
to venture through a crack at midnight

beaky the Master looms biting limelight
just in this spot guessed and for sense
evaded I'll work an idea over cliffs
not curtains by a skeleton abbey
youngman goes out sees girls
one tries to kiss him not on
lips but throat Old Count
interferes — Rage Fury
— This man belongs
to me I want him
prisoner for a
father time
told after
Bram's
bud

André Breton Dreams the Walk
of Charles Maturin

A little before midnight
by the café window
one comes out from a passage
(has that body a wolf's coat?)

greenish smoke wraps the hand
that writes on stained marble
the House must fall
(it doesn't look like a plume
it looks like a dagger)

> three wipes of a rag
> and the menu changes —
> not a flagon to pour
> or a matchstick to chew

> the square piano gives
> a heretic laugh
> no kitchen Richard
> stalks this dame-crossing lane

centuries are marked on the plate
not hours, the pavement staggers
the stamp on a packet, toys salute
as the drain floods back

did I forget to climb the stair
and deliver the text for today —
adventure startles through a ribbon
of little torments
the giant key points how

Terror Twilight

Don't need the rattle of bones
      to tell the timer's ticking
Don't need a stain on the rug
      to smell who's been before
Don't need a rusty key
      to scan the hidden passage
Don't need a blank in the mirror
      to feel the stuff drained out
Don't need a lamp in the tower
      to know the planes are coming

There's new killer waste in the living-room
as a genie spins with flicker and static

A cyberspirit crashes the website
pulling his knife on a safety platform

A scratch letter forms on the girth-rim
hissing from ragged gauze

Clutch your mobile, hug the wall
hide bottles and cans

Unplug and tune in
may use data for marketing

The keeper who saves your bacon
is the ogre who steals your face

Uncollected

2003

Forty-nine comes Clare

i.m. Ric Caddel
13 July, 1949–1 April, 2003

Gleams, a dragon eye
  over the border

lozenge against bar
  climbing

like a canon taken up
  by darker strings

Lend your ears, a psalter
  fool goes out

who birds knew inter-
  laced in columns

where water winds
  about stone

browning a tune
  part to part

This is the sack
  on the shoulder

that would conjure
  a kingdom

as the library hums
  be green her leaves

Don't ramraid the tome
  's motley

they would annex
	your very cells

where the compass face
	is a clock

a shaft broken
	away from day

forgotten of the foot
	that passes

Letter into letter
	north pressing

will deal the card
	yields sweetness

Bone Metallic

What story   holds here
pebble-human   half polished
a little piece   every contour learnt
to gross up   and win at point of chisel
a curve of hill   mossy crag with mine-shaft
or stark fault   this is home a childhood
for bluff recall   mother lamp-light lode
bearing on throne   care sturdy as long neck
reaches from shoulder   a castle tower over ward
never to admit what strain   has some trench to scoop
then further cleft or cave   so comes a pierced skull
better absent belief   all in mustard haze
under night flare   sings quiet by day
a bolder legend   not after a medal
just pull comrade   it'll count as much
when shorn limbs speak on plinth
a dale myth there t'remember
the force drives on afresh
where tube sleepers
go abstract in green

Uncollected

2006–2007

Baseline Eldorado

1

Open my heart
there the great devil
says come away, beats a path
west, far out through golden corn
to cactus desert and spine chill heights
as blue promises a lyric splash for any day

two Jacks define the mood, a red ampere light
on the dashboard — miles from burnt-out empire
where in a cul-de-sac under grey rain the tea leaves
settle, cosy to embalm just a flicker of spangled rhythm

2

Done in the morning before the other
 Two or Three . . .
who's to figure the story, that is
 pulp design

the bullet belt is a pinball machine
 how I used to laugh
I am Loopy the Loop, the Good Wolf
 don't you remember

she shakes her hair in arabesques
 by a bright red wall
she starts to put on a nurse's smock
 finds a flayed head
under gauze with google eyes

She in the trenchcoat's the heroine
 but how do you know
she fells him with a blue shoe
 drives into the future

Disney plus blood means the characters
 retail each other's words
bang BANGggggg — the speech bubbles
 hold only question marks

3

Reality isn't Verity
she wears a pubic wig
to be licked

get what you want any time
half the price it's made

elsewhere
stone barefooted

down one mean street
he walks alone

the credits get smaller
as the headlines scream

THAT COULDN'T HAPPEN HERE
(massacre or rising)

some of my best friends are
sure they didn't vote for this

tonguey ads for black juice
to fire the whole damn show

4

Folksy-dumb
the boss says
all those guys
want to steal
our neat deal
when we just
want to help
steer demo-
crazy custom
as Coke can
stop the noes

5

Is smartness
    American
        for forgery

      we are
    an elastic
country

          the Range Rider
            Cisco Kid
              stay in blood

              unaccountable
         as a rattle
      snake

you hunt
    the splatter
      cell

      behind
    your own
movie

        when nothing
          informs
            the box

           offers
        endless
      choice

so the Hittite
    pilgrim
      hammers

      the other
    lush
situation

6

They're us, that's all
against glass
of must-have
graspers and gulpers
one more
in Fox casual
a circle saw
swing-slide
keep on coming

features pressed
a viral army
megavolt
all I want's
flesh to gnaw
makes you fight
down airless aisles
lardy slabs
and turn to trash

What
by letter and tag
god or slave
drives
the cloud of knowing
on sandstone crags
is a clash of steel
to get at spice

the desert repeats
itself
as a glistening star
in a tent
calls
there is no light but Light

a last world
will not let go
played tit for tat
when your collateral
is my excuse
the video from the cave
(hello central)
jives some forsaken pelvis
out on the range
where with a zigzag scoff is need

Two Shots at Intolerance

for Tom Chivers

Oilentrance

I
Nickel
Tread
Offscum
Lorn
Except
Ricochet
Answer
No
Cavil
Enough

Nilracetone

Icon
North
Tribe
Outcast
Linch
Epithet
Raps
About
Neighbour
Cross
Entail

Kensal Gravure

I

Green lung or leaning dinosaur
walled between road and canal

first before Highgate and Nunhead
when bodies pushed out the need,
hatched after Père-Lachaise

classical over gothic
porticoes declare
as the northern terrace colonnade crumbles

straggly bushes and sky-bent trees
ruffle any square intent—
ALL SOULS lizard to linnet
quirk whatever shape is fixed

high over water the ground dips
(some cannot be known)

a long view strutted by Goldfinger's relic
smiling again
and the corbelled Italian stage
of the Hospital tower

spectral gasometers (do they still serve)
clutch arms over rusty torso
seeking Sunday storage

trains hurtle, hoot over bolts and bars
(witness to loss in the cutting)

barges hug the bank, Hero, Virgo, Maddy Rose
linger in bed all day

no talk but the birds
across space (seventy-seven acres

plus thirty-five of ST MARY'S)
or just a gardener hums

obelisks, columns, caskets, sepulchres,
winged angels, sphinxes, crosses

brick vaults down a catafalque
where brass studs and velvet
kept the boxes bright

II

One angle caught, everyone is here:
Dickens wanted this rest,
a garden shut off from disease,
the Duke of Sussex forsook Windsor —
'what an escape to such air' (1843),
Hopkins walked up past the Plough
humming a polka

not present and ever featured
in freehold lots,
goblin-sunk or proud
in dressed rubble

their names trace a maze of endeavour
mocked by bomber and vandal,
time's quiver and smear

III

Ainsworth (who reads?) a spindly urn
over fossil block, here as yore *nah fur off*

Babbage (number-engine refused)
fills a gabled granite ledger

Brunel — plain Portland block in gravel —
faces west, the public work says all

𝔚𝔦𝔩𝔨𝔦𝔢 ℭ𝔬𝔩𝔩𝔦𝔫𝔰 from bluebell patch to cross
scans the self behind

ℭ𝔯𝔲𝔦𝔨𝔰𝔥𝔞𝔫𝔨, bust gone over base,
abstains thirty years while steeling terror

𝔇𝔞𝔯𝔩𝔢𝔶, faint mark on flat stone,
stutters sums what cries for music

𝔏𝔞𝔡𝔶 𝔉𝔯𝔞𝔫𝔨𝔩𝔦𝔫 — vault 61, Catacomb B —
sends five ships for a stitched hero

𝔥𝔬𝔬𝔡, pink pedestal, bust and relief stolen,
dreams sudden blows that won't go still

𝔏𝔢𝔦𝔤𝔥 𝔥𝔲𝔫𝔱 (evergreen on marble)
chants liberty, any handout allowed

ℭ𝔥𝔞𝔯𝔩𝔢𝔰 𝔞𝔫𝔡 𝔉𝔞𝔫𝔫𝔶 𝔎𝔢𝔪𝔟𝔩𝔢, weathered ledger,
carry the old inflection into modern time

𝔄𝔲𝔤𝔲𝔰𝔱𝔞 𝔏𝔢𝔦𝔤𝔥 — vault 29, Catacomb B —
dares not breathe a name by day

𝔐𝔞𝔠𝔩𝔦𝔰𝔢, gabled granite,
frescoes the Lords after Snap Apple Night

𝔐𝔞𝔠𝔯𝔢𝔞𝔡𝔶 — vault 96, Catacomb B —
growls like a tiger, musk at the grille

𝔄𝔫𝔫𝔞𝔟𝔢𝔩𝔩𝔞 𝔐𝔦𝔩𝔟𝔞𝔫𝔨𝔢, grey slab beside her lawyer,
defies rank to expose a crime

O'ℭ𝔬𝔫𝔫𝔬𝔯, octagonal spire with broken tip,
reclaims the field for Devil's Dust

𝔕𝔞𝔱𝔱𝔦𝔤𝔞𝔫, (nameless) cross over trellis work,
keeps the lid on rolling text

Sax Rohmer, black marble as fit,
conjures a chinky scheme

Mary Seacole, palm trees and drape over slab,
lacks four yards of bandage, pillows a gashed head

Princess Sophia — sarcophagus on a tall podium —
dodges her father to get a child

Thackeray, York slab within iron poles,
darkly draws a puppet laugh

Thompson (Francis) — spiky leaves on chest —
charts the long arcane he does not tread

Trollope, staged base with cross,
writes to the hour, a pillar box of thought

Varley, headstone lately laid,
draws a spirit out, counterproves the visit

Louis Wain, under father's leaning stone,
maddens a cat's eye might be near

Waterhouse, words gone under wreath,
wants the gaze that warms in ice

Lady Wilde (private, without a mark)
longs for some rocky coast

IV

Business closer than chiselled rock
pokes out today
at the south-west edge

a damp, sealed envelope beneath a bunch of lilies
marked 'John William Waterhouse'
contains a poem in Spanish
with signature and abode (Malaga)

message for a man who left
no letters or journal,
who quietly worked his myth
from a nameless model

she stokes a brazier to raise a protective plume,
seeds, leaves and juice to coiling shroud
transfuse the ochre scarp and floor

body charged with wand and sickle,
Anglo-Saxon in orient dress
she might make young
by graving
any withered frame
this decade can throw up

poster-proof with eyes hardly vacant
the eighties obscured
speak through the sixties
to now, a little starved of exotic

an old story you believe, backfolded
when Nino *thinks* in paint

V

They are making a film in the Circle
(one van and crew) furtive as Orton
near the one-legged lion

what is it, what plot number
takes out of tunnel vapour
defiant teeth, bones and hair

SAINSBURY'S on a raft
is just permitted (cabalistic technology)
over miasmatic bubbles

this quadrant of the heart
twitches/bulb pressed into soil
stirs/noun goes verbal

ready ever to be
beyond tables bleached
actors try their parts and business

sparkling synapse rolls
tricktrack the site confined
from void to feature (stamp for repeat)

VI

X. Y. Z. —
Alphabet disperse
to show
the mass squeezed out
(them in pit or mound)

jumbled parts without a name

some less than grand
are cast in tilted book-slabs
and scattered paper roses
(IN MEMORY OF —— WHO FELL ASLEEP)

know-shall, house-all
grin/grain
scrawls in black earth

Pair a' dice by way of
stiff won't fail to find

World Levered on One

for Peter Riley

A smock. A shed. Tilting shelves. A scrap of bone with scratched lines. Glasswort in a jar. Inkblots on the table. A Floyd sleeve behind anglepoise. Set of *Perfect Bound*, incomplete. Soprano Lol with recorder echoes. Personality in things to hand.

Slip into poetry. There's no gain in a lash of progress, crowded words in a huddle, sensation-stanzas. Watch what goes on. Barnack blocks to red-streaked brick. Willows overhanging a gravel path, the river's curve. Make a record of plants, eaten or avoided. Spiky, slimy, silky. Maybe skip what allegory wants to tell.

Fresh delves by chance or choice. Intention not to fit when all at last obeys. Undulate leaf, rain-flushed. A sunshiny moment out of sullen fits. A charm for thorn pricks. Gate motet. Baffling corridor where a cycle stands. Area railing spears. Memory of other passages and ritual past decorum. In a city of towers and courts the road beckons. What scope for terms demoded. To walk is to write, the stamp it would puzzle to improve.

Birth from horizon to map with smoke and steam. Near-stopped nerve in the northern hub. As if fed through cot bars a darting artillery. Never forget those shadows. Dream an unchained body marching to a sweeter tune under torn and bannered clouds. Spots cohere in waste, wilderness. Hollow trunk of an oak with withered arm. Dies into earth to be plucked, with shells white as dog's teeth. That eastern print asks where, tug of woods or sea. A bittern booming in the reed shaws. Railway sleepers, well tarred, over the dyke between marshes.

Little knot of word-forcers or great dispersed band, down the years, across territory. We reads a version of I. Stranger-mates who chafe, dispute, revel with meat, wine and fire. Cluster to bring the still, solo act into gutsy, holy jabber. Precious stock, pressed or helped into view. Corantos, intelligence, running-on *Relations*. Some in trust will make the poem better. Faces gleam in the room upstairs, defying speakers for the thing itself. Regulars, wits and bums weigh the founding sentence. And quiet by letter as on stark paths the probe of life goes on. A gift of breath to mark an occasion, a figure of notes to bless or curse, a prospect on turf, the ordinary unexhausted.

Playing Policy Blues

With regard to the question now occurs
refer to the previous state (figures different
or the dress says so). Who drew the dome
didn't go for flickery logo but staked a gateway
some handsome ape might follow
even when disappointed his pager calls.
All teeth and ears trouble won't stick
as the rules change, exploded from nineties
to noughties. Er, y'know a domestic fellow
throws money tightly, pleasing key shooters
under blind trust. It's a double act
to offset carbon prints or tag a suspect
God-drawn. Don't think to move
on a lie, mother, hand on history's dial.

Snatch It Back Blues

Cheers some hooted, the stony heart
to shake and brace a lolling dream
vented, against all seeming habit
of me-first you-win tenders. Cleaner hands
with a speck of decent dirt would steer
the fuggy wagon along what's given away
to get health stuff back. Cool ladyland
brings in a guitarist for street cred, sings
how to sort the squabbling crew, over here
and over there. Mission grants licence
to meddle, a faith chorus richly argues
and on the rebound cuts her own
with a nail or gag. Knowledge walkers
face a stunt a week warning: don't bite that.

Policy: a daily lottery in which participants bet that certain numbers
will be drawn from a lottery wheel. (*Webster's Collegiate Dictionary*)

from The Canting Academy

2007

Decacord for Knaves

i.m. Bill Griffiths

I think, therefore it is/cracks the picture/lilies, cliffs, snow
must be taken/manifold/to know a swan/how it steers, cants
upping back by scent/as crow, nonesuch, ebony/out of nought/
give the frame to get at coal.

Sable bigots, ermine doomsters/drink every pertickler
to put away/with fine-spun reason (or sortilege)/a fellow
who faces the wall/by voice of parchment, precedent/as might
a skull in the mirror slow-butt.

Yr worship/ham a bad hand at righting/near bone-foundered
I falter/know it's not — a withered leaf, a crimson stain/is it
was it/goes mixtymusty/don't sap my brain/like you
was working a mine/scrows deeplier the gaffe.

Is this a syllogism?/James Harris committed murder/that man
is James Harris/Therefore that man &c./We assume the person
has [X] character or class/but this is just to repeat the same
in other words/Whose stroke comes over 'always'?

All (crossed) or alone/could tell of myself some business
when the stories come from another/that ordinary
secret sinner/deals a blow for the decent half/expels
bile and slime from the coil of tenement chambers. So.

What draws pity when the Law cries rigour?/The case
will be turned and tossed/with fighting on the edge
to fill a dozen bins/You'll tread a cubit nine years
or nearly/a body converts as the situation re-Quires.

Stuff that disagrees will tally/to the smallest detail/
a chair leg is a gun/moby is a witness/the mug translates
quivering lines/rid sum (write some)/down to the bore
till a spirit climbs out/carbonado traces.

Truth replies with convenience/the figure in charge
by design or accident of birth/pushes to diffuse
the stock/for sense/you could call on the first traveller
who passes/wouldn't be a bump-up official at least.

Dissect and you may find a heart/bravoledge'n'beroguetif
won't wear it/ferking a common manufactor or delinquem
with a primineery/here to direct the sewerity of justice/open
pored/if stretched/a long answer expect over a life (shortly).

An affidavy man might scare/out in the street/comes in
to the landing/becomes a dock/the scoundrel once
removed/now togged up with a velco grin/demands to settle/
summons my likeness/magnified/its Mark-master to snuff.

Uncollected

2007–2008

Proxy Features

1

Dear Alan, all the poets
are wearing T-shirts and trainers
and this is December.
There's no more Saturday night.

They drink bottle-browed
and raise the tail of each sentence.

Rob Cowan tells me what to think
but I listen thirty years back
to Aspects of the Blues
and Byrd at Ingatestone.

Francis Wilford Smith and Cormac Rigby
speak in the crevice, stuff that might as well
be here. A train pulse cut down the neck
strikes double iron, takes water on the fly.
Booker slides into Byrd and a babe
embattled in brick, burning
cries joy through viol engagement.

Someone checks their mobile, another
pings away to get a picture. The buttons I see
get smaller. My drifting ear catches a verse
of Purple Heather somewhere below
the garble. There's only one speedo
on the scene holds his heart and why
be him? Across the abstract flatland
a bevy of recruits is tagging
the screen says Hi, thanks for this. It's easy
to slam and what we know seems right.

Little cases can't avoid the hiss
but may disclose some shiver in space,
an oxide print of a moment

coaxed back from dawn, flavour and scent
along corridors to a metal frame
perhaps with echo. A chinagraph
plotted these turns, a punchy phrase over slack
tuned drums. You remember and expect
but the instant isn't the one
over your shoulder, it's somewhere ahead.

Ah, Martin tells me he teaches rhetoric
in Idaho, even a snatch of Auden
before he left. What's ruled out
in the great dispersal claws a hold,
skill that stiffened till it had to be chucked
only to lose the tilt between speak
and beat. Life can't be a silly trick
but childwords depend, come through
ribs in a spotted leaf.

2

Out of war or the next heroic
we bear a dual stamp, doomed
to kick against the harsh stead
that gives us a measure of ease
and driven despite to build
a glassy frame which all can climb—
green in lingering dirt. If this
is a lungful before the break
it's done to pitch an argument
forward. Our history is walking
on the page, from ridges to fields
with clumps and laid hedges of thorn.
Any marvel drawn on wire lines
will call up a force to survive.

Can't get careless in a lane smothered by plastic
or a thorium-steeped stream. Don't like to fix
what is right for health and who knows
some plants and creatures may return. Still

there's a way to behave which allows
adventure and doesn't tie the lurching
spirit. A feel for the scape of things —
prepossession and extension. In which heave
there's a deal of home-coiling at staggered
remove. You're in the scene you create
shaping and stained, little sensations
a cue to shuffle then remark.

Ground, air, water
and their minuter properties
at an angle in stark habit
surprized. To see in the fibres
of a name touched and familiar.
Tussocky grass and a tumble
of crooked stones. Starred in summer
by flagrant bedstraw, millfoil, knapweed.
Windswept tower, silent except
when shaken with the great voice of bells.

3

Agnate forms disperse and intercross —
slash-black snail to whirling sky
serpent to growing stalk
louse to cleaving tree.

Fret-strokes from kernel
unfold, flecks stormwrung
in slithy shock-wet sloggering
burst the brain-cage to vent raw wit.

Where's the pilgrim
can chart alive these tremors and rollicks?

Maggie makes the words perform
even to bleeding breath (switch-swatch
interrealmic filch and tangle)
in vertizontal sleepscare turns

round a paper garden diddy voscus
goes the hound-horse alley aster
goes the bull-cat pomerlastus
goes the fish-bird umper umper
through wily slots down yew-scarp alleys
whole in the wanting account.

Geraldine in this same room
pendles a greenish white meteor.
Its slow curve over black scalped crags
a year off in wellmarked motion
carries brightly over a bare stretch
where drabber voices slink. Far located
she tonics the present den, as mariole
traces glint from a window scratch:
Ya ta tethera mithera mock, lata slata
hevera devera dot. Mysterious so
ivories and vibes in jangling talk
hover then hit hard, flatted sideways,
ostinato rise and dip.

4

Now a happy proser
pulls the drape. His movie might
be adverts. Wouldn't wish to smear
the April scroll — to sound like yourself
is a strange meander. And yet that's just
how the blacktop score evolves.

It's a good-for-nothing ear
that'll not hear how a dance is done
before any instrument. Bare instinct
prods the nerve and bone into play, later grunts
will tally.

Dream on the wall at waking
just a step beyond eyelid pictures.

The poems come slower these days
as a body of years tiered deep
settles into focus.

Inside the noughties
wars are buried while feel on demand
piles goods into the arena —
see them now you don't burns a signal
that hurts with promise
wanting to cheer but fetching up sour.
There's always more
to learn or try, this is the core business
getting a shape and throb
in some ordinary jaunt down the road
under a given sky.

5

The lamp above flickers. Streaks blot
bilious wallpaper. A beer ring on the table
shows how writers relate. When did we
have tidy rites? Out of the sludge
a vital draught is brewed and spills
a bit that lingers. Sense trails after
rhythm tapped — drip drop over intent
a profile gathers. The soundhole is an eye
rumorous at midnight, taking us in
beneath strings, unsmooth. Dizzy bar
set for chronic speculation.

Good company's a baize surface
where balls shoot into the net. Expertise
jostles with rude abandon. An aspirant clutches
the rod, hungry to bounce off the hero
who — a lifetime or half ago — started a frisky
seeming duffer. Welcome as heir
a smile might say or is it an invite
to stick at zero. Petty feuds die in the pocket
then revive: passed-over versus fêted,

curiously flat versus curiously inflated,
articles attached versus light-grip spielers.
So much is staked in the choice and place
of a term, you might not want to engage
as this mildmay winter could scourge
the bravest poking bud.

Worlds on a pinhead dazzle, spin, kiss,
jump, collide. Late night philosophy
cuts an I to an H, so anyone might think
they can't live in the same room, the same air.
But there's a fleur-de-lis on Butcher's Row
and every banjaxed inkslinger
will hug an impish figure, golden devils
spliced. Our magic is got from scraps
and without an edge of menace—
clubbable gives it away—the matter
won't spring. At bottom it may be
the poet plays him or her self
getting to the state required. Which means
the tribe that clusters here, present or remote
is an engine of support, likelier than appears
will stand a crazy test.

What lyric feasts have gone down
and goster steered to a ragged chorus.
Not an actor's project, rather the maker's
mouth-marks, sometimes mumbled,
singular to the text and that occasion.
So often we've ventured the newest fare
breathed, warmed, ignited. Given or bartered
the first-struck pages, before any slender board
seals composure, to turn
in air, mindskip the gap more difficult
to delight. How we hit things by chance
and kept in the groove, returning
from a spun alphabet to space and silence.

6

It's time to sign off. You know the score
of a casual career seriously done. We push
the pieces caught at the instant running
into a fit. Patterns begun out of limbo
like a pat on the head in childhood
beaming through generations
will implant such care and zeal, a sketch
to follow then discard. Not to be too mystical
the skull, the veins fill with letters cognate:
Graves back to Queen Anne, via Swinburne,
Landor and Johnson — in a sandy walk
on Wimbledon Common. Or again by A.C.S.
to Wordsworth at Rydal Mount — the elder
admitting some good might be had
in the work he'd leave. Translate lakes
to sea, an enthusiast hides an addict.

Your *Lives*, which crave a fifth season of store,
press into brief this honey and salt
stalking to the margin what quirks excite,
more Aubrey or Wood than Great Cham
except for the poet's (literal) eye. A routine
of book sorts can incline the gaze to rivet
our moving world, the sound steeled
from ages shed. You sift remains
to gather the stunned terms that bite
as if to talk a life over
won't square. Unbuffed fragments
keep converse and lie true. Grey features
quicken to colour, filter-luminous,
a sonagram yielding another ghost
in the tableau. Forgotten, remembered,
they assert their share today, tuned
a little different to entice.

I'll clear the stockpile now
and just say you meet those spirits

coming up the stairs like bees —
no truck with any -ite or doxy
or bossed crew that staves the range.

You dress as suits the part, now without tie,
ready to break a code and lock the basics
into their sharpest form. Fashion that counts
is a capital hand leading the vowel
and its garments. Untranslatable fabric, black
lodged in white. A spell below chat
is a little map and yours between rendezvous
zigzag, dodge directorship — squibs
let off to reach and re-spark the field. With this
there can't be an end but a poetic agent
whispers in the glass of red
over and out.

Deep Clearance

for Lee Harwood

It starts early, the way we read the world —
the whole complex, blood and setting,
points like a map.

                   What's this picture
debossed, three men with a pistol
meting justice to hangdog forms by a tree?
The Castaways by Harry Collingwood
an English prize for my father,
Christmas 1928, Devon House School,
Margate.

                His copy of *The White Company*
with detached boards, signature and address,
184 Wardour Street, my own name
appended above.

                  Stories from English History,
my mother's prize, September 1927,
Lady Margaret's School, Willesden Lane.
'No more wars', says the parson in hope
(last page).

               The Wonder Book of Railways (1921),
'ninth edition — almost entirely new',
driver's view as a green steam train
approaches a tunnel.

                 Pyle's *Book of Pirates*,
not lost to a jumble sale as thought but here
with all its plates commending 'deviltry':
'Would not every boy rather be a pirate captain
than a Member of Parliament?'

And on
to *Dangerous Waters*, a 'Senior' prize (1960),
man overboard in Atlantic gale, MG chase
over Exmoor, London bank vault heist.

Scottish Folk-Tales and Legends, 'all ages'
might spark the giver too. Wicked queen
at the window in purple dress. Tam Lin,
Thomas the Rhymer, stuff to summon
a guitar.

Welcome dread these jackets speak
like *High Sang the Sword* — a Viking ship
with dragon prow, Irish tunics tagging
the boys who watch.

'So I got the other hand',
frontispiece of *Lorna Doone*, his grasping hers
through a grille.

Can Balfour cling to a spar
before the wrecked Covenant in a large octavo
Kidnapped?

Sherlock Holmes (complete),
M.R. James (complete), assorted Haggard
and Buchan.

A page falls open, surest trawl —
'She sang Roxolana's song . . . it would be
exciting to hear [her] in another seven years.'
(Geoffrey Trease, *Trumpets in the West*)

Dusty, mottled, a little damp, yesterday's stock
starts to realign. All margin
each book a case of unwritten thoughts.

Up from the Vault

For the Christmas holidays of 1920-21 I had invited a boy called
Richardson to stay with us. . . . [He] had wasted several shillings on
magazines, [including] the *Picturegoer* . . . which [had] articles . . .
about making films, including one about, I think, the Stoll Studios at
Cricklewood . . . This was for me! I never had the slightest doubt that
I was meant to direct films from that day to this.

Michael Powell

So it was Raleigh.
'Props! Ready with the potato,' shouted the assistant. . . .
A scurrying little man in a check shirt ran in to the set.
'What the devil have you been doing?' cried the director.
'Peeling it, sir. . . .'

Joan Morgan, *Camera!*

Re-run book or play
        jacket off

mostly silent comes monumental

> *Melody of Death/Passionate*
> *Friends/Four Feathers/Wheels*
> *of Chance/Wandering*
> *Jew/Sign of Four/Prodigal*
> *Son/Woman in White*

disowned where 4x4s park
by Matalan's long frame,
bottles and wrappers
on the grass verge
down to Oswald Terrace and Stoll Close

Nothing to tell now
under metal hulk or safe box rows
which won't expose
another fabric

blank-nerve likeness, near and remote

The Temple estate
 viz. hereditaments conveyed, 1903
 by Rt. Hon. Helen Mabel, Countess Temple
 & Capt. Chandos Graham Temple Gore Langton
 below the Cricklewood (railway) curve
 west of Edgware Road

to the Bush Electrical Engineering Co.,
 whence Nieuport & General Aviation Co.
 and Smith's instruments

A busy site, World War One
 as the Nieuport Nighthawk
 replacing the Sopwith Snipe
 comes off the line

Jump to a GB patent, 1918
 for fuselage framework,
 its cross members and gussets
 fixed without bracing
 wires and bolts

saving skilled labour and material . . .
but the factory closes, August 1920

So steps in Stoll, 'Sroswald'
 SHORT TAKE OFF AND LAND
 a block-of-granite sort of chap
 in frock coat and top hat,
 theatre man
 from the Coliseum and antipodes

A vast brick hangar with tall windows
along Temple Road
to propel scripts to screen,
its stages able to manage
five on the go at once

Correctly costumed, scaped and spoke

a crook, revolver in hand,
acetylene blower in the other,
smashes a safe
while monks walk in procession
under Gothic arch
and Lady Di (Manners)
on a Stuart four-poster
fends off the villain

Successful fare comes in bits
when your public needs a hook

Adventures of Sherlock Holmes

familiar from the last rolled out
in prolonged life —
Norwood with the author's seal,
tobacco, disguise and violin
fools even the studio,
shell of his chambers, face and innards
caught for a better likeness
in mercury vapour

Hound of the Baskervilles

Norwood again with brooding eye,
fierce-cut profile on the moor
(Hampstead Heath) at sunset,
the hound silhouetted black on blue,
its aura — flickering white fire —
scratched on the negative

The Mystery of Dr Fu Manchu

fifteen two-reelers, including —
the scented envelopes, clue of the pigtail,
the fungi cellars, man with a limp,
the queen of hearts, shine of seven lamps

Then hard on heels a supplement—

>midnight summons, the coughing horror,
>Cragmire tower
>
>clutching hands of the Devil Doctor
>Harry Agar Lyons
>with eyebrows shaved,
>skull cap and chung-sam,
>arrives Irish via Chinatown
>
>true London green exterior
>crossed with stock sets
>amber inside
>and Fu's speeches in yellow type
>throughout

Action and variety
makes phony beside the point
as garden lizard plays giant centipede

Shooting Stars

>between two dull vehicles
>(Stoll within Stoll)
>the real story runs
>
>crane-shot she walks, a vamp
>from horse-opera set
>to slapstick comedy
>
>*he* has found ideal mate/*she* kisses
>his best friend/loves all her fellow
>workers/the chorus girls laugh
>
>now found out
>the only thing is to swap
>the prop, a shotgun loaded live
>(bullet spirals through air

and the right wrong man falls
from a chandelier)

Whatever happened to Mae? She's
an extra in a thirty-bob crowd
while her old partner (man and star)
shines in the spot

Work any hours on the great conveyor,
one all-nighter every week,
no going off except for privy relief

Factory of art, two floors with a deck above,
all tasks from carpentry to cutting
done on site

Labyrinth of memory rooms,
enamel, concrete, steel, as 'L' outspread,
its heart a tableau bright in dim space
pumping a dream for critics to judge

Slag off the whole business
ashamed of greasepaint
forgetting invention
and it hardens by *close-up* to truth

Claw yellow/Quixote/wanders
Wastedale/on Broken Road/Greatheart
Confessions/isn't Everything/the Girl
of London/River of Stars/One Arabian/
One Colombo Night/not for Sale/
by Machines that Think/clicking
Blinkeyes/to meet/Fawkes/Turpin/
Froggy's Little Brother/Becket/
Boadicea/Lochinvar/the notorious
Mrs Carrick/Aliette Brunton/
Sally Bishop/at Long Odds
like Guns of Loos/no False Evidence/
just a Glorious/Further/Last Adventure

The British film
a faint embarrassment—
dark leather before dark wooden panels
propping a classic, As Is
that would rather be football

Stoll, stodge, still (*a thorough job*)
from peak to slump
the tarnish sticks (*sequent fit*)
over dynamo hood

So what's different, as America floods
the scene, friend and foe
by long reach? Easy to grift
balsa blimp and free-base dollies
do the same war in laughs
rising to any sop (it's only
the only language bends a little)

All sold off in a three-day auction,
cameras, miles of cable and flex,
carriages, cloaks, goblets,
rights to a cabinet of stories,
and with a heave the site itself

What's left in the pile of nitrate
(Elvey, Asquith and Coleby)
cries to go in a carbon arc
seventy years through glass

Think there's nothing and then you see
the miniature Oswald Terrace (1990)
is bolted to an end-wall fragment
of the Stoll empire, a looming slice
cream against brick, still as before
attached to no. 2 Temple Road,
Edwardian or thereabouts,
almost a camera trick

Uncalled back, just here
the real unreal thing
caught in risk-instant
of partition, sliding
to engage

Dialogue over title
in dream-bubble, twin-pram screams
by traintrack hush, chips strewn
among tall blue flowers, aerosol perfume
from pink curtains, lone trolley
on pavement corner

    Now the world of model repeat
    LLOTS bare LLOTS alive
    grafts its warm promise
    on to a field of bones

Index and erase
to recompose —
a sentence never finished

Gulf Ghost File

for Geraldine, Nether Edge swimmer

Didn't think
        when I rooted here
of the Welsh Harp
we walk to   over fortress hill, circular traffic—
the Brent river dammed
        below the join
        of Dollis Brook and Stream Silk

Now I turn out of the house
        down a slope
to the main road
where once I saw   down a manhole
the brook converted
        twelve foot down
        that cannot take today's rain

Rendell's latest
        has a dank summer
of drizzle and storm
and in mind at least   the Harp
bursting its bank
        to force a torrent
        south to Portobello

I read Sam Charters
        on New Orleans—
'proud to swim home'
says a bumper sticker   recall
my gris-gris soak
        by Pontchartrain
        from Rampart Street in the heat of '68

Could use a nilometer
        the one I saw
Elephantine in 1990

to measure the height   of this floor
above the V
            of the Slade's
            long stream-bed road

            Swish of a skirt
                  hints god-sip
            unrefrainable
murmur and gush   O what would
the cledge be
            reft of outwelling
            secrets we find ill-come

Crickearl's Chorus

But cantos oughta sing

Jack Kerouac

               Air-tossed Hope & Anchor
                 on highroad slow
                    over radio flares

cookney
   mal-lingo
     race-rush
        jagga-bite
          freeboots
            pull to a point
            in brute spice
scarce all the world could reach, birds, hills, streams
by spade mark, spectre or no, this mottled grindscape
                   here
                   it draws
                   further on
                   it spores
                   around
         in strips between brick and stone,
        secret squares, valley cup or mound
             anodour

baby lorn
rancountered
     charlock
     mayweed
     sun spurge
             tower slabs
             sparrer pipes

     an archive dream
     re-rumbles
     to laugh

Duometric

for Frances (again)

You light touch the scene
                    pencil detail
                    from path & field
                    nimbly scatter
                    word roots
                    by scent
                    of stone or bird
                    on page

I reach by ghost trek
                    in buried stream
                    for that logodrift
                    floats the story
                    pieces   can
                    stick   rag
                    weed   as
                    folio score

We walk the garden in these streets
my late your early comes in exchange
a discant ajoine, charging each
                    letter found
                    leaf-line
the tongue wraps around
with a decade plus of still go play
from burgundy to dark green, spaces
that allow the primal dance another gleam

They has a ribbon turn to reveal its verso
as little clues of (L) inkage
make in these stranger parts a home

Divisions on a Ground

$\qquad\qquad\qquad\qquad$ *Awake*
$\qquad\qquad\qquad$ my Eyes
$\qquad\qquad$ at Night my
$\qquad\qquad$ Thought[s]
$\qquad$ pursue
$\quad$ you[r]
charming Shape
$\quad$ and
$\qquad$ find it
$\qquad\qquad$ ever new
$\qquad\qquad\qquad$ if my far
$\qquad\qquad\qquad\qquad$ pressed
$\qquad\qquad\qquad\qquad\qquad$ Eyes
$\qquad\qquad\qquad\qquad$ to sleep
$\qquad\qquad\qquad$ resign
$\qquad\qquad$ in crazy
$\qquad$ Dreams
$\qquad\qquad$ your Voice
$\qquad$ and Perfume
$\qquad\qquad$ twine

$\qquad\qquad\qquad\qquad$ ache or ape
$\qquad\qquad\qquad\qquad$ I leap
$\qquad\qquad\qquad\qquad$ ink
$\qquad\qquad\qquad\qquad$ wine

$\qquad\qquad\qquad$ ought-arm-in-ver-
$\qquad\qquad\qquad$ sign-oice-met

$\qquad\qquad\qquad$ Wake$\quad\quad$ Night
$\qquad\qquad\qquad$ caught$\quad$ Shape

$\qquad\qquad\qquad\qquad$ yes/am
$\qquad\qquad\qquad\qquad$ dear
$\qquad\qquad\qquad\qquad$ to/raise
$\qquad\qquad\qquad\qquad$ 'nd
$\qquad\qquad\qquad\qquad$ rest

Codacrop

Stay with light
in crypt
as poet crashes

just what's left
        of heart
attend for sure

tune deep dug
as muse
shall entertain

there he offers
        by her
dream-thread

dim over flash
a canny
shot can move

strange at first
        it then
may convince

richer as shard
that air
means to grow

Notes and Acknowledgements

The arrangement of texts is basically chronological. However, 'Star Carr' has been shifted from its notional place in *Azimuth* — after 'Greenhouse' — to a point near the beginning of the book. Sections of *Roxy* (written 1985-96) have been placed after the two books of sonnets written between 1987 and 1991. Poems from the period covered by *Azimuth* (1972-84) but not included in that book have been allotted their appropriate position within the sequence, otherwise reduced. These out-takes were subsequently published in *Puzzle Canon* and in the magazine *Figs*. A shorter version of 'Hammer Pond' was printed in the signed, limited edition of *Azimuth*. Two extra poems from the *Days of '49* project sit alongside pieces from the book itself. For reasons of length and overall unity, no material from *Hymenaei, Amergin, Epithalamion* and *Vitagraph* has been selected.

A few texts are presented in revised versions, the changes usually resulting from reading conditions and hence long established. Radical alteration of three early poems was incorporated in the first draft of *Music's Duel*, put together in the early 1990s, and the book retains these forms. One piece, 'De Luce', appears here in its near-original state and in its 1990s incarnation (used on the CD *After Hour Shoots*). Several unnamed poems have been given titles, partly to prevent them being lost in the mix.

Each of my books has a distinct structure and it has been a challenge to extract material from its original context and create a coherent thread across a longer span. Where texts form part of a book or sequence it has always been my assumption that, beside local function and particularity of reference, they should also work as individual units. I hope that both possibilities remain in the current instance. A representative selection of work from each period is provided, although, given the overall format, it did not seem feasible to reproduce some of the more experimental texts, such as 'Wormenhert' from *Azimuth*. Unpublished and/or uncollected pieces have, in various places, been chosen in preference to more available matter.

* * *

Scope (Gr. *skopein*, to watch, consider) charts the view from the house on the German-Danish border where Emil Nolde did much of his work, including the 'unpainted pictures', executed in secret during the years 1941–45 when he was forbidden to paint. **The True Generation of Serpents** is taken from a pamphlet in the *Harleian Miscellany*, vol. III, and a note in *Folk-Lore Record*. The probable derivation of **Knucker** (i.e. knucker-hole, Sussex dialect) is OE. *nicor*, water monster; cf. Icel. *nykur*, water-horse or sea goblin. **'What did I do'** includes reference to Elgar's Sussex retreat, Brinkwells, where the Piano Quintet and Cello Concerto were completed, and quotations from his letters. **Untitled** is a response to the practice of Jackson Pollock.

Shandy Shivers is inspired mainly by Sterne's fantasy about a spirit who frequents the ruins of Byland Abbey (see his letters and *Journal to Eliza*). **Transmission** attempts a Chinese linguistic structure. **Of Mausolus** arose from a visit to a regular haunt, Castle Howard, when I gained entrance to Hawksmoor's Mausoleum through a door left open by workmen. **Versipellis** fuses the Norse outlaw type (*berserk* or 'wolf-coat') with the fabulous origin of 'turn-coat' in Pliny, *Natural History*, VIII, 34. **Dreads and Drolls** evokes Notting Hill in 1883–86, as experienced by Arthur Machen, and draws on writing undertaken there or concerned, retrospectively, with this area. The slogan in *Southam Street*, section III, later used as a book title by Ken Livingstone, was taken from graffiti on a nearby bridge.

Metabasis was triggered by a visit to Berlin shortly after the fall of the wall. *Danse Macabre* refers to the woodcut of a printing office in Matthias Hus's edition, 1499, which contains the earliest known illustration of a printing-press. Part of the context for **Capricho Oscuro** is Cervantes's landing at Denia and subsequent stay in Valencia, October 1580. **Red Light on Green** draws on the BBC *Variety Programmes Policy Guide for Writers and Producers*, the so-called 'Green Book'. **ManU/Mersenne Primer** concerns the computer or 'Automatic Digital Machine' built at Manchester University, where Alan Turing contributed to a seminar on artificial intelligence (both 1949). **A Line Engraved** alludes to a 1948 walk by prominent MPs which anticipated the National Parks & Access to the Countryside Act (1949) and also to Nicholas van Hoogstraten's attempt to block rights of way on his Sussex estate, 1999. **Vortex**

Rerun follows Frances Yates's interpretation of the relationship between and meaning of the two Luttrell portraits.

Tomogram is an enquiry into the origin and meanings of 'ghost', including its use in a printing context. **Faded Novel: Fine Again** is a distillation of the relationship between *Finnegans Wake* and J.S. Le Fanu's *The House by the Church-yard*. **Exquisite Corpse** juxtaposes quotes from Le Fanu's *The Room in the Dragon Volant* and Frances Sheridan's *History of Nourjahad* in alternate lines. **Duelling Tales** refers to the elopement of R.B. Sheridan and Elizabeth Linley and the duels Sheridan fought with his 'rival' Captain Mathews, the whole business recorded in conflicting accounts. **Exercise for Ear**, a 'shortest day' text, was loosely prompted by the heroines of Elizabeth (Sheridan) Le Fanu's *Lucy Osmond* and Stoker's *Dracula*. The two parts of **Criss Cross: In Irving's Shadow** draw, respectively, on the writings of Algernon Blackwood and Bram Stoker, who apparently met in 1893.

Up from the Vault concerns Stoll Film Studios, the largest in Britain (1920–38), where noted directors and technicians learnt their trade, inventing key devices. The filming of 'English Rose' in Joan Morgan's novel takes place at the (unnamed but vividly described) Cricklewood site. **Gulf Ghost File** refers to the Slade Brook, which runs underground from Cricklewood Broadway (Edgware Road) along much of Anson Road before joining another tributary which flows into the river Brent. The base text in **Divisions on a Ground** is a song by Sir Charles Sedley.

* * *

Given the context of this gathering, it seems to appropriate to indicate some lines of influence. My father had various poems by heart and recited them to me when I was a child. My mother was much interested in visual art and cinema, and passed on a love of these forms. One uncle was an artist and architect; another was a mining engineer. Early enthusiasm for history and archaeology resulted in an inclination to read the present through the past. I began studying law at university and this probably contributed to the dialectical nature of my work. Readers may detect signs of absorption in Renaissance metaphysical poetry, Melville, British poetry of the 1940s, and writers associated with Black Mountain

College. Beyond this it may suffice to mention the impact of the London poetry scene from the 1960s onwards.

* * *

Thanks are due, in particular, to the following:— as sources of inspiration and support, Kristine McKercher, Beryl Popplewell, Jill Florent, Angie Riches, Sheralee (Parker) Purcell, Shakti Temple-Smith, Anne (Brock) Cooper; as commentator and collaborator, Alan Halsey; as publishers, Michael and Mark Ziesing, Alison Meyers, Alan Halsey, Paul Green, Peter Hodgkiss, Bob Cobbing, David Annwn, Glenn Storhaug and Tony Frazer; as computer programme advisors, Patrick Lee, Ken Edwards, Dona McCullagh, Glenn Storhaug and Neil Crawford; as keystone to the whole, through years of difficulty and delight, my partner Frances Presley, without whom this project could not have come to fruition.

* * *

Original book publication details:

Playground for the Working Line (Ziesing Brothers, 1981)
Azimuth (Binnacle Press, 1984)
Puzzle Canon (Spectacular Diseases, 1986)
Strip Signals (Galloping Dog Press, 1986)
Elizabethan Overhang (Spectacular Diseases, 1989)
Southam Street (New River Project, 1991)
Tilting Square (Binnacle Press, 1992)
Roxy (West House Books, 1996)
Danse Macabre (Ispress & West House Books, 1997)
Days of '49 (West House Books, 1999)
Le Fanu's Ghost (Five Seasons Press, 2006)
The Canting Academy (Ispress, 2008)

Thanks also to the magazine editors, too numerous to list here, who printed much of this work before it was published in book form.

Lightning Source UK Ltd.
Milton Keynes UK
24 May 2010

154629UK00003B/7/P